CASES IN ADVERTISING AND MARKETING MANAGEMENT

CASES IN ADVERTISING AND MARKETING MANAGEMENT

REAL SITUATIONS FOR TOMORROW'S MANAGERS

EDD APPLEGATE AND
ART JOHNSEN

ROWMAN & LITTLEFIELD PUBLISHERS, INC.
Lanham • Boulder • New York • Toronto • Plymouth, UK

ROWMAN & LITTLEFIELD PUBLISHERS, INC.

Published in the United States of America
by Rowman & Littlefield Publishers, Inc.
A wholly owned subsidiary of The Rowman & Littlefield Publishing Group, Inc.
4501 Forbes Boulevard, Suite 200, Lanham, Maryland 20706
www.rowmanlittlefield.com

Estover Road, Plymouth PL6 7PY, United Kingdom

British Library Cataloguing in Publication Information Available

Library of Congress Cataloging-in-Publication Data

Applegate, Edd.
    Cases in advertising and marketing management : real situations for tomorrow's managers / Edd Applegate and Art Johnsen.
        p. cm.
    Includes bibliographical references and index.
    ISBN-13: 978-0-7425-3835-1 (cloth : alk. paper)
    ISBN-10: 0-7425-3835-4 (cloth : alk. paper)
    ISBN-13: 978-0-7425-3836-8 (pbk. : alk. paper)
    ISBN-10: 0-7425-3836-2 (pbk. : alk. paper)
    1. Advertising—Case studies. I. Johnsen, Art, 1944– II. Title.
HF5823.A7935 2007
659.1—dc22   2006014844

Printed in the United States of America

⊚™ The paper used in this publication meets the minimum requirements of American National Standard for Information Sciences—Permanence of Paper for Printed Library Materials, ANSI/NISO Z39.48-1992.

CONTENTS

FOREWORD

LEARNING CRITICAL thinking skills to make sound, logical decisions while working in some area of advertising or marketing can be achieved by studying and analyzing cases, especially if the cases are based on actual situations or experiences. This book features 46 cases that should appeal to students and their professors. The first 40 depict situations that have occurred or could occur in various kinds of companies that are different in size The last six cases summarize important elements discussed in the previous cases and provide additional information pertaining to advertising and marketing, including descriptions of advertising and marketing positions often found in advertising agencies and in companies.

All of the cases allow students to experience what various employees, especially those in managerial positions, have been confronted with. Each case encourages students to develop well-reasoned solutions to the problem or problems raised. Indeed, these cases provide students with the opportunity to apply the principles and concepts appropriate to advertising and marketing that they have learned in previous courses.

These cases are interesting, current, and concern a broad range of advertising and marketing problems pertaining to consumers, advertising agencies, and companies, including profit and nonprofit. They cover topics such as positioning, media strategy, budgeting, sales promotion, P-O-P, personal ethics, professional ethics, marketing planning, integrated marketing communication, creative strategy, SWOT analysis, PEST analysis, global marketing strategy, brand management, pricing, e-commerce, acquisitions, mergers, segmentation, targeting, buying behavior, B-to-B marketing, objectives, tactics, services marketing, direct marketing, forecasting, distribution, promotion, advertising opportunity, advertising planning, marketing research, advertising regulations, and agency compensation.

The cases vary in length and difficulty. Some require more thought than others. Nonetheless, the questions following the cases encourage students to offer in-depth analyses, no matter what the length or difficulty level of the case may be.

Joseph R. Pisani, Ph.D., Professor Emeritus
Department of Advertising
College of Journalism and Communications
University of Florida

ACKNOWLEDGMENTS

WE WOULD LIKE to thank our colleagues for their help during the writing of this text, especially Dr. Joe Pisani, who was kind enough to write the foreword and contribute a few cases to the text. We would also like to thank our students for their analyses of many of the cases making up the text. Their comments and thoughts are greatly appreciated.

We would especially like to thank our wives for putting up with us while we conducted research, wrote the cases, met deadlines, and performed our jobs.

Most of all, we would like to thank the wonderful and varied world of advertising and marketing for providing the rich fabric from which this book is cut. Throughout the cases, readers will meet interesting and infuriating characters, highly motivated people, everyday and unusual situations, and occasionally a situation that seems too stretched to be real.

The people attracted to these two disciplines—advertising and marketing—are the stars of this book. To these bright and colorful people, we say, "Thanks."

Edd Applegate
Art Johnsen

THE CASE METHOD

The case method offers students an opportunity to apply what they have learned in previous courses to "real" situations that happen in business. Usually, a case focuses on a problem or issue, and you must identify the problem or issue and provide a reasonable solution. Coming up with the latter requires careful analysis of the case.

Read each case at least twice. The first reading is to learn what the case concerns, the basic situation. The second reading is to analyze the information so that you can develop a rational and logical solution or course of action.

During the first reading, you should ask a series of questions. What is the major problem or issue? Are there other problems or issues? Who are the key people and what are their positions? What is the professional environment in which the key people work? You should read the questions at the end of the case before doing the second reading, because these questions will help you think about specific elements of the case. Be aware that the problem or issue may not be obvious. In fact, the problem or issue may be hidden by facts and other information. In the "real" world of business, problems or issues are often misidentified or overlooked.

During the second reading, be aware that the case contains facts and other information, and that the facts may be incomplete, inconsequential, or misleading. As you read, identify the significant facts of the case; more importantly, try to determine the fact's meaning. Pay particular attention to information in exhibits, especially those with numbers. Monetary figures, if present, should be seriously considered. Of course, you may need to put yourself in one or more key people's shoes in order to understand the person's behavior or decision. Be careful not to confuse symptoms and causes. Avoid rush judgments. Do not assume that what the key people did or suggested in a case was the correct course of action or the best decision. People holding managerial positions sometimes have to take action or make decisions based on little information. Sometimes these actions or decisions are not the best actions or decisions.

Whatever you suggest to resolve the case, whether it is a solution or course of action, should come about after much thought and commitment. You must weigh the consequences or ramifications of your decision or suggestion. Also, the decision or suggestion should be stated carefully. If you recommend some action, then state that action in precise terms. Include details about what is to be done and how.

SUGGESTIONS TO FACULTY

Students should be encouraged to present their analyses of the cases in class. The following procedure is merely a suggestion to help faculty who have not been teaching courses in which cases have been required.

Instructors may ask students to:

1. Restate the important facts mentioned in the case.
2. Evaluate the actions or decisions mentioned in the case.
3. Identify the goals of the organization or the objectives of the individuals mentioned in the case.
4. Present the existing problems or the problems that are likely to occur based on information in the case.
5. Present a solution or course of action to the problems mentioned in the case.
6. Present alternative solutions or courses of action to the problems mentioned in the case.
7. Weigh the advantages and disadvantages of each solution, alternative solution, and/or course of action they suggest.
8. Predict the outcome of each solution, alternative solution, and/or course of action they suggest.[1]

Consequently, the above material can be presented as the following:

1. Statement of the facts.
2. Statement of the problem.
3. Statement of the causes.
4. Statement of the solution or course of action.
5. Statement of the alternative solutions or courses of action.
6. Statement of the decision or recommendation.

In the world of advertising and marketing, an idea or position is only as good as it can be presented, articulated, and defended. Having to "get on your feet" can be a powerful learning device that will develop confidence and presence. Not all students will like this aspect of the case method, but for those who do, and for those who accept the challenge, their other classroom experiences will be brought to life.

Finally, students can, and will, learn as much from their classmates as from the instructor through the case method *if* the instructor is prepared to *lead* the class discussion but not dominate it. The more students are able to discuss a case among themselves, the better.

NOTE

1. This list is adapted from Kenneth E. Schnelle, *Case Analysis and Business Problem Solving* (New York: McGraw-Hill, 1967), pp. 27–28.

PART I

The Business of Advertising and Marketing

Smith Services, LLC
When a Client Doesn't Pay on Time

ONE OF THE roles played by every ad agency president or owner is that of "collection agent." Depending on the business you are in, the kinds of clients you have, and the economic conditions that surround you, more than likely, at some time in your business career, you will have to call a client to ask why your invoice has not been paid.

Over the years, the answers clients have given have become standing jokes:

"The check is in the mail."
"The dog ate the invoice."
"I thought we'd paid that."
"We paid that last week."
"The invoice is being processed."
"The bookkeeper has been on vacation."

Sometimes clients stretch out payment as long as they can to improve their own cash flow. This, of course, can jeopardize the agency's cash flow. Sometimes sloppy procedures on the client's end cause invoices to be lost. But no matter the reason, usually, as a final resort, the president or business owner owed the money has to call the client's company to start a conversation.

Most ad agencies purchase an off-the-shelf computer software program such as "Clients and Profits."™ This software allows for a completely integrated system to track individual job costs, keep track of Accounts Receivable, record Accounts Payable, allow jobs to be scheduled through production, and provide reports for agency management that give information on everything from monthly Profit and Loss, to year-to-date financial performance, to the status of each and every job in the agency. While such operating software can be expensive, it is essential to providing a framework for managing an ad agency's daily life and financial situation.

Each month's end, or as frequently as needed, the agency's Finance Department can use "Clients and Profits" to provide:

- An Income Statement showing the month's financial results, and results year-to-date.
- A Balance Sheet.
- An Accounts Receivable List, by client.
- A Client Invoice Aging List.
- A Key Indicators Report that shows, on a cumulative monthly basis, current year versus previous year company performance regarding:

> Assets
> Accounts Receivable
> Investment Account
> Cash Operating Account
> Accounts Payable
> Accrued Expenses
> Sales
> Gross Income
> Expenses
> Year-to-date Profit/Loss

VICTOR JAY

As the president of Shoemaker, Inc., a small design firm in Arkansas, Victor Jay studied the month-end reports produced by "Clients and Profits." So far, through the first six months of the year, his agency was doing well financially. Sales were up 15 percent over the first six months of the previous year, expenses were about the same, and gross income and net profit were up. The Investment Account was growing, and most important of all, the Cash Operating Account was solidly in the black and growing. This was all good news.

But all was not perfect.

Victor studied both the Accounts Receivable list and the Accounts Receivable Aging List. It was standard policy at Shoemaker to ask (and expect) clients to pay invoices on receipt. But over the past three months, two of Shoemaker's major clients were not paying as promptly as they had been. Client #1 was now paying about 45 days from the Shoemaker invoice date rather than within 30 days, as they had been. Still, there were not any past due amounts.

Client #2, on the other hand, was a different story. Just short of $13,000 had moved into the "90 days" category on the Aging List, while $22,000 was in the "60 days" column. This meant that Client #2 was 60 days past due on $13,000 and 30 days past due on $22,000. Even more troubling was the fact that Client #2 had only partially paid against the total invoiced amount each month.

To Victor this signaled trouble. When a client "cherry picks" a statement, and only pays selected invoices, it can mean they are having cash flow problems. Client #2 had done this two months in a row. Why hadn't this client paid *all* the invoices due? Why had they picked only a few to pay? Was there a reason attached to the ones chosen for payment?

When a client is in trouble financially, it is not unusual for an ad agency to be the one whose payments are withheld. Generally, a client in trouble will pay vendors for what it needs (raw materials, inventory, etc.), and expenses such as advertising get moved to the bottom of the payables list.

Client #1 was a fairly new client to Shoemaker, and they had told the agency that they intended to spend significantly more in the next fiscal year than in year one.

Client #2, Smith Services, LLC, was a longtime Shoemaker client. Actually, Smith was Shoemaker's first client, and they had been with the agency for more than seven years. Victor had been unaware of any payment problems at either client, but now both situations caught his eye.

VICTOR'S NEXT STEP

Victor reached for the phone, and then he stopped. What should he do *right now*?

QUESTIONS

1. Whom should Victor call first? Why?
2. Should Victor make the calls himself, or is there someone else who should call from the agency?
3. What should be the tone of the conversation between the agency and each client?
4. What are the risks to the agency if Victor (or someone else at the agency) calls? and if he does not call?
5. Whom should Victor ask to speak to if he calls?
6. What if either or both clients don't pay in full in the next 30 days?
7. When should Victor get his lawyer involved?

2 Guys and a Girl, LLC
Intellectual Property Law and Other Legal Matters

WHAT COULD be more exciting than fulfilling a dream that has been fanned by the spirit of entrepreneurism for more than five years? Bill Wagner, Dave James, and Elizabeth Charles, all previously employed with other companies in junior marketing or advertising positions, finally decided to take the plunge and start an advertising agency. They had talked about it many times while in college and ever since their graduation two years ago. The name of their ad agency, 2 Guys and a Girl, was the name they had decided on one late night in college. They knew that use of the word "girl" might offend some, but they also saw it as distinctive, so the agency's name was sure to be remembered. Besides, they all liked the reaction they got from most people when they first heard the name. The surprise was furthered when people learned that the "girl," Elizabeth Charles, was the company's president.

Even before the company existed, Elizabeth got a friend to create artwork and design a letterhead and stationery for the enterprise. The three partners wanted to see what others would see when they eventually went into business. They liked what they saw.

Using savings, advances on their credit cards, and some money from their respective families, they opened the doors to 2 Guys and a Girl Advertising in rented space in an old factory loft. They were able to secure "we three" as their phone number (938-4733) and wethree.com as their website domain name. Their initial client roster was somewhat thin, but they knew they could count on doing work for Bill's father's company, Wagner Manufacturing, and for David Jones's brother's retail store, Hollywood Baking and Bread Company. Another client was Elizabeth's sister, a chiropractor with a growing business.

Ownership of the agency was split evenly among the three founders. They agreed that if anyone left the agency, the other two would buy the shares of the departing partner. But none of them could ever imagine leaving, and they all knew that once they were successful, they would laugh at the details and other non-advertising mish-mash they had to go through to get started. In fact, the ease with which it all happened made them think nothing was impossible.

THE CLIENTS

The Wagner Manufacturing Company (WMC) made salty and sweet snack foods. Most of its sales were to distributors in the United States, but a growing demand for these types of products had WMC looking to Europe and Asia. WMC had an annual advertising budget of $100,000 that paid for packaging design, trade ads, in-store displays, business-to-business promotions, and entertainment.

Hollywood Baking and Bread Company was a single-unit retail store and restaurant that sold specialty breads, sandwiches, and other lunchtime fare. Located adjacent to an upscale mall, Hollywood Baking was just starting to turn a profit on monthly operations. Competition for the female lunch crowd was intense, however. Within the past few months, two similar upscale restaurant concepts had opened in Hollywood's general market area.

Dr. Kathy Charles, Elizabeth's sister, was part of a two-person chiropractic office located in a strip shopping center at a high visibility location. Dr. Charles, an aggressive, driven individual, was a strong proponent of "pushing the envelope" in her ads and promotional activities. She believed in the curing and rehabilitative power of her chosen profession, and she wanted to take on medical doctors directly. In fact, some of the advertising ideas that she showed to Elizabeth were pretty confrontational to the M.D. community.

THE CLIENT'S CREATIVE IDEAS

Since all three of the agency's initial clients were "family," some interesting dynamics came into play. All of the three founders were younger than their client contacts, and this led to no shortage of client-inspired ideas and opinions. WMC wanted to run comparative ads in Europe and Asia so that potential customers could clearly see the differences in their products versus those of the competitors. And, because in-store promotions had been so successful in the United States, WMC wanted to do the same in Europe, particularly in France, where it was known that a "sweet tooth" existed within a majority of the population.

Hollywood Bread wanted to do a guerrilla marketing campaign targeting area shoppers. Why not hand out flyers in the mall, do some street chalking, have a plane drop leaflets, and do an outrageous outdoor advertising board that would generate controversy and make an impact on the lunch crowd it desired? The creative idea behind the campaign was "We Serve Ordinary Shoppers, Too," a headline designed to overcome the perception that the deli catered only to "svelte, sophisticated, BMW-driving women."

The outdoor visual featured what appeared to be an overweight woman taken by an amateur photographer. Other print ads featured pictures of famous Hollywood stars, and Hollywood Bread's radio commercials used impersonations of stars' voices to recommend the restaurant.

Dr. Charles's ideas were the scariest of all. She was aware that controversy could improve the fortunes of a business. This, combined with her naturally aggressive personality, led her to give Elizabeth the following four headlines for her first campaign:

- "If he can't stop the pain, I can." (A picture of Dr. Charles accompanied the headline.)
- "Tired of pills? Why not try competence?"
- "Pain management? It's not taught in most medical schools."
- "Spending more money than you should on health care? What a shame!"

2 GUYS AND A GIRL

The doors were open, and the ad agency they had dreamed about was in place. WMC, Hollywood Bread, and Dr. Charles were all successful businesses that were now clients. The agency was ready to begin work when Elizabeth asked, "Does anyone think we should check with our lawyer? Advertising in Europe and Asia, celebrity endorsers, and my crazy sister's ideas? I'm scared to death."

QUESTIONS

1. What are the potential legal issues for each client's campaign?
2. Do you see any legal issues that the agency, as a company, faces?
3. What issues are involved with clients who are also family?
4. What position should the agency take with its clients' suggestions?
5. When, and where, do you think 2 Guys and a Girl should start discussions with legal counsel?
6. How should the agency prepare to talk to its lawyer?

Harrison Advertising
Growth Strategies

FOUNDED IN 1990, Harrison Advertising had emerged as one of North Carolina's most successful advertising agencies. With a staff that totaled almost 130 people in 2001, the agency was seen as a creative powerhouse, where great ideas, one after the other, flowed in seemingly endless fashion. All of this great work was based on smart and strategic thinking driven by forceful and relentless founder Chris Harrison.

In fact, the agency was a constant contender for "Agency of the Year" at both *Advertising Age* and *Ad Week* magazines. Chris was in constant demand as an authority on everything from "effective advertising" to "how to build a great ad agency." From an account base that saw first-year revenues at only $7 million, the agency had grown in just 11 years to $84 million in billings by the fall of 2001.

It was at that point that momentum began to stall.

With the economy already feeling the pinch of a gathering downturn, the tragic events of September 11, 2001, took place. Much of Harrison's business came from clients in the travel and tourism segment. With vacation travel, especially by air, decreasing, and with hotel and resort bookings at near historic lows, Harrison's clients acutely felt the impact of a changed world.

Within 18 months, two of Harrison's competitors in Raleigh closed their doors. One of these ad agencies had been experiencing severe cash flow problems for some time, and its closing was not unexpected. However, the shocker was the closing of Allen+Allen. After Harrison, Allen+Allen was the next largest ad agency in the city.

Louis Allen and Chris Harrison had worked together in New York. The two friends moved to Raleigh, N.C., in 1988 and formed Harrison & Allen amid great fanfare and high expectations. After some success in attracting several former New York clients, the two had a "falling out," at which time they divided the clients and the agency and established their own individual ad agencies.

Over the years, the bitterness and difficulty of the breakup diminished, and Louis and Chris enjoyed a professional and respectful relationship with each other. Their agencies, however, competed "tooth and nail" for every possible new account, every creative or industry award, every good employee, and even on the softball field and basketball court. It was said that the competitive spirit of each of the principals was such that they got up each morning just to better the other. It was generally accepted that the competition between the two men was in part responsible for the success of both agencies. Competition has a way of making everyone better, and no one knew this more than Chris Harrison.

The closing of Allen+Allen really unnerved Chris, and it raised many issues both good and bad for Chris to consider. But first, he had to find out what really happened at Allen+Allen. Should he call Louis Allen and just ask him? Should he ask some of his staff, many of whom were friendly with their counterparts at Allen+Allen, to see what they could find out?

Already, Chris and his Human Resources director were being inundated with calls from former staffers at Allen+Allen, asking about opportunities at Harrison. Even though Harrison Advertising didn't plan to hire additional staff at this time, should Chris use their interest in Harrison as a way to find out about what *really* happened at Allen+Allen? Should he instruct his H.R. director to find out all she could through arranging interviews with former Allen+Allen personnel?

While musing over what to do, Chris's phone rang. On the other end was John Lantor, one of Chris's senior account people.

"Chris, I have a friend of mine, Bill Penick, in my office. I think you might want to come down and hear his story about what happened at Allen+Allen. We've been friends for a long time."

Chris took the stairs two at a time to Bill's office. One hour later, all Chris could say was, "Wow."

WHAT BILL PENICK TOLD CHRIS HARRISON

With the events of September 11 and the economic recession, Allen+Allen began to suffer a series of seemingly unrelated small setbacks. As with Harrison Advertising, clients became wary and cautious about their spending plans for 2002. Many of Allen+Allen's clients, feeling the slowdown, started to reduce staff. This further eroded client spending as the uncertainty of 2002 set in.

Advertising has always been a business where agency managers and owners are willing to add staff and resources to meet client spending patterns. But, as spending decreases, agencies face the painful step of laying off staff to decrease monthly overhead. This can lead to a downward cycle of events in which everyone is trying to cut expenses rather than build business. That is what happened at Allen+Allen, where a general "business malaise" set in.

If there is one word that describes many senior people in the advertising business, it is "optimistic." Optimistic that their agency will survive. Optimistic that they will find a solution soon. Optimistic that whatever downturn they are experiencing is only temporary and a rebound is only a day or month away.

As 2003 approached, Allen+Allen started to look at alternative strategies for growth:

- Should they acquire another advertising agency to improve their cash flow?
- Should Louis Allen sell Allen+Allen to a larger ad agency in order to have access to more capital and financial strength?
- Should he sell the agency and retire to Florida?

As Bill described it, Louis Allen looked into all of these options. He also looked into drawing on his bank line of credit and agency credit to sustain operations until "things got right."

Hoping to remain independent, and full of the optimism that many successful agency entrepreneurs possess, he decided to "stay the course." He, Louis Allen, and his agency, would ride out the storm and come back with a vengeance in 2004.

In January 2004, Allen+Allen's largest client declared bankruptcy and closed its doors. Then Allen+Allen's contract with the State of North Carolina Tourism came up for renewal. With a diminished staff, Allen+Allen tried to defend its position for contract renewal. The client, still angered by the loss of several key agency people, chose another agency for the next four-year contract period.

Next, a series of staff resignations and defections made it difficult to service the remaining business. And the downward spiral continued.

Unable to face a growing list of creditors, with staff defections increasing, with cash flow at a new low, Louis Allen tried to sell the agency to several of the former suitors, but most didn't even return his phone calls.

Out of time and out of options, Louis Allen closed his once successful agency to minimize any further losses. Everyone in the Raleigh ad community was saddened and shocked.

CHRIS HARRISON'S NIGHTMARE

As he walked slowly back to his office, Chris's mind was racing. *Was it even possible* that Harrison might be headed for the same fate that Allen+Allen experienced? Harrison's account list was not long, but while the agency didn't have as many clients as Allen+Allen, they had always been solid financially. Harrison's staff didn't seem like they were restless and "looking," but who knew?

What if . . .?

Chris knew he had to consider his options once again. He didn't want to wind up like Louis Allen, not in control of his company's fate as it spiraled downward. With more than 95 employees counting on the agency for their livelihood, with financial obligations to meet, and with the desire for a comfortable retirement after so much hard work, Chris made a list of his options.

STAY THE COURSE

Chris could try to ride out the economic downturn and decreased billings. His agency owed little money, owned its own building (actually, Chris owned it), his clients seemed stable, staff morale seemed high, and cash flow was positive and being managed well. There was no reason to expect something calamitous would happen, but Louis Allen had felt that way only months earlier.

"I've always trusted my instincts, and I've always been lucky. I'm going to throttle expenses back a little more and wait for better times. I'll give it six months more."

MERGE THE AGENCY

Molly Duncan, CEO of a small rival ad agency, had approached Chris six months earlier about merging their two companies. One of the benefits of doing this was that Molly's account base was not travel or tourism related. But it consisted of only four very large clients. Molly's company had 40 people on staff and appeared to be doing well. Maybe this was an option . . .

SELL THE AGENCY, BUT TO WHOM?

Chris knew that any number of national agencies were interested in opening a branch office in Raleigh. He felt that with a few well-placed phone calls, he could get talks started with someone interested in buying his agency. If he took this route, should he ask to stay around for a few years to manage the "transition?" Or should he seek to cash out as soon as he could and retire so he'd have more time to play golf? He had close relations with some of his employees that went back years. What would they think? How would he feel?

One final possibility was to offer to sell the agency, over time, to either a small group of Harrison employees or the entire staff. This would take time to work out, time that Chris felt he had, but he wasn't sure.

There is a saying in the ad agency business that "Most agencies are three phone calls away from bankruptcy." Every time Chris's phone rang, he wondered if it was call "number one."

Put yourself in Chris Henderson's shoes.

QUESTIONS

1. Look at each option Chris identified. What are the pros and cons of each possibility?
2. What further questions would you ask yourself?
3. How would you pursue each of the above options?
4. What would *you* do?

The Koch Brewing Company

FORECASTING SALES can be difficult. Usually, forecasts are made for a brief period, such as part of a year or a year. However, forecasts for longer periods may be made for research and development or production purposes. Generally, the marketing manager is responsible for developing sales forecasts or overseeing the department that has been assigned the task. Of course, sales forecasts will be used by others in the company.

Basically, a sales forecast is an estimate of how many units can be sold during a specified future period based on a specific marketing plan and an assumed marketing environment. According to J. Paul Peter and James H. Donnelly Jr., a sales forecast has several important uses:

1. To establish sales quotas.
2. To plan personal selling efforts as well as other types of promotional activities in the marketing mix.
3. To budget selling expenses.
4. To plan and coordinate production, logistics, inventories, personnel, and other areas.[1]

In short, a sales forecast can be an invaluable instrument for several departments within a company, not just the marketing department. Benefits from a sales forecast include the following:

Information about consumers, including their buying habits.
Information about when and how much to order.
Planning for production and capacity.
Identifying patterns or trends of sales.
Determining the value of the business.
Determining the expected return on investment.

All of the above information may result in:

Increased revenue.
Increased retention of customers.
Decreased costs.
Increased efficiency.[2]

There are different methods or techniques for sales forecasting. These can be mathematical (quantitative) or based on sales force estimates (qualitative). Mathematical methods or techniques include causal models and time series models. Causal models such as correlation and regression are used to determine a relationship between sales and a variable or variables presumed to be related to sales (for instance, advertising). Time series models use historical data as the basis for estimating future sales. Such models include moving averages, exponential smoothing, and extrapolation. Qualitative methods or techniques include judgment or subjective models such as the executive judgment method, the sales force composite, and the Delphi method.

THE CASE

The Koch Brewing Company, Cincinnati, Ohio, is not far from the downtown area and the Ohio River. The company, which began as a microbrewery, offers consumers several kinds of high-quality beer distributed to various retailers and restaurants in a tri-state area covering southern Ohio, northern Kentucky, and southern Indiana.

Janice Brewer has been working as the company's marketing director for five years and is responsible for developing short-term and long-term sales forecasts as well as marketing plans. At the request of Laura Simons, vice president of sales and marketing, Janice completed a long-term sales forecast based on sales for the past five years. When Laura stopped by Janice's office to have a look at the report, she smiled and nodded her approval. She realized a long time ago that she could depend on Janice, no matter what she asked of her. "Very good. Everything seems to be in order. Will you have your presentation ready by tomorrow morning?"

Janice nodded. Laura had asked her to present her sales forecast to James Koch, the president of the company.

"Great. I'll see you in the morning." Then she left.

Janice sat there and looked at the document. Then she glanced at her watch; she had three hours to prepare her presentation on PowerPoint before she was supposed to meet her husband after work. She wondered if she should call her husband and tell him that she may be late. *Not yet*, she thought. *I have three hours.*

Janice finished the PowerPoint presentation and glanced at her watch; it was fifteen minutes before five. She had fifteen minutes, so she proofread the PowerPoint presentation.

The next morning Janice presented her sales forecast to President James Koch and his staff (see table 4.1 for her projections).

"For the sales forecast, I examined our sales to distributors for the past five years and learned our sales had increased each year by 5 percent. This figure is the average. As you can see in the handout in front of you, sales increases were less than 5 percent in some markets and more than 5 percent in other markets. Then I looked at the current year's sales figures, which average higher than 5 percent. In fact, the average is almost 6 percent."

"What about the next three years?" James asked Janice.

"Well, as you can see, sales should increase by more than 7 percent each year."

James turned to Laura Simons and shook his head. "Laura, is there anything we can do to increase sales by at least 10 percent a year over the next three years?"

Laura nodded. "Janice is working on a marketing plan that calls for more advertising, which is something we have not been doing enough of."

James looked at Janice. "How much more money do you think you will need for advertising?"

"Well, as you know, our advertising allocation is rather low, considering the size of our market. In addition to asking for several hundred thousand more dollars for local television, which covers our market, I am asking for a few hundred thousand for nontraditional, alternative media. I may suggest that we hire female college students to promote our brands in various venues throughout the tri-state area. They could dress in outfits that promote our brands; they could talk to the customers about our brands."

James looked at Laura. "What do you think about that idea?"

"Well, to tell you the truth, this is the first time I've heard about it."

James looked at Janice and asked, "What makes you think you can pull this off?"

TABLE 4.1

Three-Year Sales Forecast for the Koch Brewing Company

SALES[a]	YEAR 1	YEAR 2	YEAR 3
Southern Ohio	$7,500,000	$8,000,000	$8,500,000
Northern Kentucky	$2,500,000	$2,750,000	$3,000,000
Southern Indiana	$2,000,000	$2,225,000	$2,500,000
Total Sales	**$12,000,000**	**$12,975,000**	**$14,000,000**
COSTS[b]	YEAR 1	YEAR 2	YEAR 3
Southern Ohio	$4,500,000	$5,000,000	$5,500,000
Northern Kentucky	$750,000	$900,000	$1,000,000
Southern Indiana	$500,000	$650,000	$750,000
Total Costs	**$5,750,000**	**$6,550,000**	**$7,250,000**

[a] Sales—These amounts are based on what the company earns at the distributor level.
[b] Costs—These costs are for the production and distribution of the products.

"Well, college students are eager to work, especially in restaurants, bars, and night spots that appeal to young people. Just look at what they've done for Miller Lite—"

"I've seen the sales figures for Miller Lite, but I'm not convinced that the Miller Lite Girls had that much of an impact," James said.

Janice looked at Laura, as if expecting Laura to say something, but Laura remained silent. Janice said, "Well, according to the articles I've read, I think there may be a direct link. Anyway, I think the idea has merit and should be considered."

"Laura, what do you think?" James asked.

"I think it may be worth investigating. However, I think we should try the regular and alternative media first, just to see what happens. If our advertising in these media work, and I mean if it causes sales to increase 10 percent or more, then we won't have to employ female college students. Of course, I'm sure that Janice will suggest in her marketing plan that we participate in the annual festival."

Janice smiled. "We can't overlook that, considering the amount of publicity the event generates and the number of people who participate. In fact, last year, based on surveys, we were one of the most recognized brands in the tri-state area."

"That's correct, we were," James said, "and I'd like our brands to be the most asked for by the most people in the tri-state area. Right now, based on sales, we are number two in southern Ohio, number one in northern Kentucky, and number two in southern Indiana. However, since Cincinnati has a long history in brewing beer, other companies may be interested in establishing breweries here, like Boston Beer did some time ago. What I'm saying, Laura, Janice, is that no matter what you suggest in your marketing plan, make sure that we hold on to our position. In fact, I'd prefer ideas that will make us number one in all three states."

"Although we are number two in southern Ohio and southern Indiana, we are gaining on our competition," Laura told him. "I think we will have passed our competition by this time next year."

"I hope you're right, Laura." Then James looked at Janice. "Janice, thanks for the sales forecast. When will you have the marketing plan ready?"

"By the end of next Friday," Janice replied.

"Good. When Laura has had time to examine it, I'd like to see it."

"Okay."

James glanced around the room. "If there's nothing else to discuss, this meeting is over."

QUESTIONS

1. Janice used sales figures for the past five years for her sales forecast. Do you think this is the best method for her to use? Why? Why not?
2. If the above is not the best method for her to use, which method is the best? Why?
3. Do you think the idea about using college females to promote the company's beer is a good one? Why? Why not?

4. If you do not think it is a good idea, can you suggest another that is better? Why is your idea better?
5. Do you think Janice's projections for each year are realistic? Why? Why not?
6. Do you think the suggestion about using alternative media is a good one? Why? Why not?
7. What alternative media do you think she has in mind? How could each medium be used to sell beer?

NOTES

1. J. Paul Peter and James H. Donnelly Jr., *A Preface to Marketing Management*, 10th ed. (New York: McGraw-Hill Irwin, 2006), p. 138.

2. "Conduct a Sales Forecast," L2S Inc., 2000. Available at http://va-interactive.com/inbusiness/editorial/sales.

International Marketing and Swanson Cosmetics

COMPETING INTERNATIONALLY presents risks for companies. Philip Kotler writes that "the risks are high," then lists several of these risks, including "huge foreign indebtedness, shifting borders, unstable governments, foreign-exchange problems, tariffs and other trade barriers, corruption, and technological pirating."[1] Before companies enter markets in other countries, they should investigate the countries to determine whether any or all of these risks exist or will exist.

In addition, companies need to understand the cultures of the countries they intend to enter. Basically, culture refers to the customs, beliefs, social norms, and material traits of a group that are passed from one generation to another. Generally, this is reflected in what the group eats, wears, and values as well as in how the group acts and thinks. To develop marketing communication plans for markets in other countries, companies must assess the countries' cultures because the cultural characteristics or traits will have an impact on brand-message strategies. Strategies will in all likelihood vary from country to country because potential customers' attitudes, beliefs, values, motivations, and perceptions will differ from country to country.

Edward T. Hall described countries as having either high-context cultures or low-context cultures. He writes,

> A high-context (HC) communication or message is one in which most of the information is either in the physical context or internalized in the person, while very little is in the coded, explicit, transmitted part of the message. A low-context (LC) communication is just the opposite; i.e., the mass of the information is vested in the explicit code.[2]

In discussing Hall's high- and low-context cultures, Augustine Ihator writes,

> In high-context societies, the importance and power of words are de-emphasized. . . .
> The perception of the message sender, nonverbal cues, social and physical contexts,
> are used to ascribe meaning to a transmitted verbal message.
>
> In low-context countries, great emphasis is placed on words. . . . The message
> receiver is expected to derive most of the meaning from the written or verbalized
> statements and not from non-verbal behavior cues, or social and physical contexts.[3]

To study cultures in 50 countries, Geert Hofstede applied four criteria or dimensions:

1. Individualism versus Collectivism.
2. Large or Small Power Distance.
3. Strong or Weak Uncertainty Avoidance.
4. Masculinity versus Femininity.

Hofstede found that wealthy countries are more individualistic, while poor countries are
more collectivistic.[4]

In their discussion of Hofstede, William B. Gudykunst, Stella Ting-Toomey, and
Elizabeth Chua write,

> The emphasis in individualistic societies is on individuals' initiative and achievement,
> while emphasis is placed on belonging to groups in collectivistic societies. People in indi-
> vidualistic cultures tend to be universalistic and apply the same value standards to all.
> People in collectivistic cultures . . . tend to be particularistic and, therefore, apply differ-
> ent value standards for members of their ingroups and outgroups.[5]

The authors point out that there is a corresponding relationship between Hofstede's individualism and collectivism dimensions and Hall's low-context and high-context categories: cultures that Hall labels low-context are individualistic, whereas cultures Hall
labels high-context are collectivistic. "It, therefore, appears that low- and high-context
communication are the predominant forms of communication in individualistic and collectivistic cultures, respectively."[6]

High-context collectivistic cultures can be found in Japan, China, France, Saudi
Arabia, Argentina, and Spain, among other countries. Low-context individualistic cultures can be found in the United States, Switzerland, Germany, Canada, and Australia,
among other countries.

There are also differences between Eastern and Western countries that affect marketing strategies. According to studies, advertisements in Eastern cultures tend to be emotional or symbolic, while advertisements in Western cultures tend to be hard-sell,
informative, practical, or utilitarian.[7]

THE CASE

For more than 10 years, James Bohannon has been the vice president of marketing at Swanson Cosmetics, a company that manufactures women's and men's products. Several of the company's brands, including its most expensive—Beauty—for women, sold well in the United States and Canada. Now the company wanted to sell its brands for women in markets abroad, and Bohannon was responsible for finding answers to the following:

1. Should the company market more than one brand outside the United States and Canada?
2. Should the company market more than one brand in the same market (country) outside the United States and Canada?
3. If the answer is "No" to the first question, which brand should be marketed and where (which markets, which countries)?
4. If the answer is "Yes" to the first question, which brands should be marketed and where (which markets, which countries)?
5. How should the brand be marketed (strategy, creative tactics)?

Bohannon thought that the company's senior management would be receptive to his decision to introduce one brand, not several, abroad. If sales were good, he would suggest that the company consider introducing a second brand abroad.

The company manufactured and sold the following brands that appealed to women in the United States and Canada:

Beauty (Swanson's high-priced brand—example, $50/1 oz. bottle of perfume)
Glamour (Swanson's less expensive brand—example, $35/1 oz. bottle of perfume)
Gorgeous (Swanson's least expensive brand—example, $25/2 oz. bottle of cologne)

For the Beauty brand, the company manufactured only perfume. For the Glamour brand, the company manufactured perfume and cologne. For the Gorgeous brand, the company manufactured perfume and cologne as well as other kinds of cosmetics, including blush, mascara, and lipstick.

In addition to examining *World Cosmetics Markets*, an industry trade publication, Bohannon searched the World Wide Web and learned that American companies exported cosmetics all over the world. In Asia, Japan, South Korea, and Australia, consumers purchased hundreds of millions of dollars' worth of American cosmetics annually. In fact, Asia was the second largest cosmetics market in the world. China alone purchased millions of dollars' worth of American cosmetics annually, and according to the China Association of Fragrance, Flavour, and Cosmetics Industry, the country had become the second largest cosmetics market in Asia. According to the association, the country ranked eighth in the world. Bohannon noticed that sales of American cosmetics to China had more than doubled in three years. Bohannon wrote the word "China" in his notebook then continued searching.

Consumers in Europe, including the United Kingdom, Belgium, France, the Netherlands, and Germany, purchased hundreds of millions of dollars' worth of American cosmetics annually. The Russian Federation purchased millions of dollars' worth of American cosmetics each year. In fact, sales of American cosmetics to the Russian Federation had almost quadrupled in three years. The Russian Federation was one of the fastest-growing markets for cosmetics. Bohannon noticed that the amount for China was more than twice the amount for the Russian Federation. In short, China was purchasing more American cosmetics. Nonetheless, Bohannon wrote the words "Russian Federation" in his notebook.

Both countries presented problems. In addition to having different regulations regarding labeling, for example, these countries had different cultures that companies in the United States, especially companies like Swanson, had little knowledge of. Fortunately, Bohannon had traveled to China and understood some of its customs.

For instance, he realized that Chinese characters are sign-symbols, unlike the letters in the alphabet used for the English language. In other words, Chinese characters are inherently meaningful linguistic units. He also understood that the Chinese language contains a large number of homonyms: words that are pronounced the same but have different meanings. Bohannon remembered talking to a marketing executive in China. The executive had informed him that characters have smaller units called radicals, which consist of two to five strokes, and these radicals have meaning, just like the characters. As a result, connotations and meanings have to be analyzed at different levels. For instance, the name has meaning, the characters have meaning, and the radicals have meaning. Careful analysis is important so that a product name is appropriate and no part of it has negative connotations.

Bohannon learned that for branding purposes, it is important for a company to use a name that can be written well. In the Chinese culture, a name is like a work of art; it needs to "look good" in written form. Basically, the name functions like a logotype or trademark. Companies need to create distinct writings for the brand names and benefits in their ads. In fact, in many ads that appear in China and other Asian countries, brand names and key benefits are positioned in the center of an ad to attract the consumer's attention.

The Chinese marketing executive also told Bohannon that a name should be "lucky." He explained that this meant a name should be balanced—that is, have yin and yang—feminine and masculine characteristics. Yin words have an even number of strokes. Yang words have an odd number of strokes. Names that are considered "lucky" have a total number of strokes that equal such "lucky" numbers as 8, 11, 13, 15, 16, 17, 18, 25, 29, 31, 32, and 39. Companies in China and other countries in Asia spend time and money on selecting names for the companies' identities and brands. In some cases, fortune tellers are hired to help with selecting names.

Bohannon realized that the Chinese, like other Asians, are image conscious. The companies that associate their brands with prestige or an upscale image and provide pleasing aesthetics have been the most successful. Companies that focus on the Chinese people's beliefs in the supernatural have also succeeded.

Bohannon understood that companies need to project a positive image, not only for their brands but for themselves. Companies need to understand feng-shui, the ancient art of geomancy (assessing the most favorable conditions for a venture). Some companies consulted feng-shui experts and publicized this in the media. Such publicity informs consumers that the companies are looking out for them. Bohannon knew that some companies designed buildings based on consultations with feng-shui experts.

The marketing executive also informed him that the Chinese value decoration. They enjoy displaying colorful multiple forms and shapes. They also value naturalism. They enjoy symbols and displays that feature rivers and mountains. Such styling is used frequently in packaging and advertising. Colors are important, too. Red is by far the most appealing color. Yellow is pleasant; it is associated with authority. Blue is considered cold; it is associated with evil. White is associated with death.

Bohannon also knew that the Chinese care about what others think of them. They are influenced by others in their reference group and are concerned about "losing face."[8]

QUESTIONS

1. If Bohannon intends to suggest that the Swanson company introduce one brand into one market or country, which brand do you think he will suggest? Why? Which brand would you suggest? Why?

2. Which market or country do you think Bohannon will suggest? Why? Which country would you suggest? Why?

3. Let's say that Bohannon recommends introducing Gorgeous, specifically the cologne, into China, because of the price. The package for this brand is approximately five and a half inches tall and two and a half inches wide. The small box is solid white, except for the name, "Gorgeous," which is one inch from the top, and a rose, which begins half an inch below the name. The rose contains a stem that slightly curves toward the bottom of the box, stopping half an inch from the bottom. The letters of the name and the rose, which are red, are embossed; the stem, which is green, is also embossed. What would you suggest about the package if you were Bohannon? Why?

4. What are some possible problems that the name, the package, the product, the price, or other aspects of the product may present?

5. If you worked for the advertising agency that has Swanson's account, what creative strategy would you suggest for advertising the company and its brand in China? Explain your reasoning. (You may need to read an advertising principles or advertising copywriting book that discusses creative strategies before you answer the question.)

6. Describe at least two ads for Swanson Cosmetics and its brand that will attract consumers in China. Explain why these ads will work.

NOTES

1. Philip Kotler, *Marketing Management*, 11th ed. (Upper Saddle River, N.J.: Pearson Education, 2003), 384.

2. Edward T. Hall, *Beyond Culture* (Garden City, N.Y.: Anchor Press/Doubleday, 1976), 79.

3. Augustine Ihator, "Understanding the Cultural Patterns of the World—An Imperative in Implementing Strategic International PR Programs," *Public Relations Quarterly* 45, no. 4 (2000): 40.

4. Geert Hofstede, "The Cultural Relativity of Organizational Practices and Theories," *Journal of International Business Studies* 14, no. 2 (1983): 78–81.

5. William B. Gudykunst, Stella Ting-Toomey, with Elizabeth Chua, *Culture and Interpersonal Communication* (Newbury Park, Calif.: Sage, 1988), 40–41.

6. Gudykunst, Ting-Toomey, and Chua, *Culture and Interpersonal Communication*, 44.

7. Tom Duncan, *Principles of Advertising and IMC*, 2nd ed. (New York: McGraw-Hill/Irwin, 2005), 674.

8. The material about China and Asia is adapted from Bernd H. Schmitt and Yigang Pan, "Managing Corporate and Brand Identities in the Asia-Pacific Region," *California Management Review* 36, no. 4 (1994): 32.

Pricing and the Model C100

AS ONE OF the four P's in the Marketing Mix, pricing can be difficult to determine. As J. Paul Peter and James H. Donnelly Jr. put it, "One of the most important and complex decisions a firm has to make relates to pricing its products or services."[1]

Indeed, if a price is set too high, customers may not buy; consequently, the business may fail. On the other hand, if a price is set too low, customers may buy, but income may not cover expenses. In this situation, the business may fail as well. Or, as Richard P. Bagozzi writes, "At the bottom end, costs provide a floor below which the firm cannot survive for long. At the top end, prices are constrained by competitive undercutting or by a ceiling on what consumers can afford or what they feel gives them value. In between lies the degree of freedom open to a firm."[2]

Whoever is responsible for establishing price plays an important role in a company's welfare. Indeed, a company depends on price to cover the cost of offering or making a product, to pay expenses, and to provide a profit so it can stay in business and possibly expand later. Yet, in many instances, individuals making decisions about price identify the costs of providing the product, or manufacturing the product, or offering the service, then add a percentage or markup to get a return on investment. Many retailers use this *cost-oriented pricing strategy*.

Generally, individuals who are assigned the task of implementing a pricing strategy should identify the goals of the company and the objectives for the product or service. According to Bagozzi, "Common options are to view price as a means to achieve or maintain market share, stimulate primary and secondary demand, increase short- or long-run profitability, signal competitors that one means business or alternatively wishes to avoid a price war, discourage new entrants, strengthen and reward intermediaries (e.g., by providing them with healthy margins), communicate value to consumers, stay within the law, or simply act in a socially responsible way."[3]

In addition, these individuals should consider the following before they make a decision:

- The target market's perceived value of the product or service—that is, how much customers are willing to pay.
- The target market's demand or insistence for the product or service.
- The competition's prices for the same or similar product or service.
- The competition's costs for the same or similar product or service.
- The company's costs for the product or service.
- The stage of the product (or service) life cycle.
- The pricing objective.

The cost-oriented pricing strategy, mentioned above, and some other pricing strategies do not consider the customer or target market. Yet the customer invariably assigns value (worth) to a product or service based on its price. Thus, it is important for individuals who establish price to understand whom the product or service is for. If the target market is not known or considered, the price may be too high or too low.

The following are some of the more commonly used pricing strategies:

Target Return Pricing Strategy. The price is determined by adding the desired profit margin to the expenses or return on investment (ROI). This is another cost-oriented pricing strategy.

Perceived Quality or *Perceived Value Pricing Strategy.* The price is determined by the value that customers have of the product or service. Usually customers' perception of value or quality is a result of advertising and/or promotion of the product or service.

Value Pricing Strategy. The price is determined by the competition's prices for the same or similar product or service.

Everyday Low Pricing (EDLP) Strategy. Generally, the price is set lower than the competition's for the identical or similar product or service to attract customers.

Market Skimming or *Prestige Pricing Strategy.* The price can be determined by the uniqueness of the product or service or by customers who are willing to pay a premium (high) price for the product or service.

Market Penetration Pricing Strategy. The price is determined by the company's desire to gain market share. Consequently, the price may be set unusually low for a certain period of time. The price may be increased later.

Competitive or *Going-Rate Pricing Strategy.* The price is determined by assessing the average price for the product or service in the market or by assessing the average price of the competition.

THE CASE

Roger Smith, the executive vice president for sales and marketing at Carpenter Motors, looked at the new model—the C100—that the company was about to release to the U.S. market. Based on the success of the C200, the 100 was a smaller version with a smaller engine. However, it contained lines and details similar to those of its big sister. Of course, the price for the 100 was relatively less, too. This was important to senior management who had supported the model. In fact, several senior executives had told Smith that his marketing efforts should focus on the car's price. Smith had thought about value pricing as the primary pricing strategy before the car was unveiled several months earlier. Value pricing, which had been used to reflect real-world selling prices and to reduce Carpenter's dependence on rebates, had worked to a certain extent for other models, but not as well as Smith had liked. Nonetheless, he was willing to use this pricing strategy for this model.

QUESTIONS

1. Would you use value pricing to introduce the C100 or any new model? Why? Why not?

2. Do you think Smith should include a rebate along with value pricing? Why? Why not?

3. If Smith uses value pricing, which is used primarily so Carpenter does not have to offer rebates, do you think he should wait before he offers a rebate for the model? Why? Why not?

4. If you are not in favor of using this pricing strategy, which strategy would you suggest? Why?

5. Do you think other companies will try to compete or counter Carpenter's value pricing strategy? If so, which strategy do you think the companies will use? Why?

6. What do you think the main selling point or idea should be in the C100 ad campaign? (Remember, the main selling point or idea should be the heart of every ad in the campaign.) Explain your reasoning.

7. Do you think the C100 may cannibalize its big sister? Why? Why not?

NOTES

1. J. Paul Peter and James H. Donnelly Jr., *A Preface to Marketing Management*, 9th ed. (New York: McGraw-Hill/Irwin, 2003), 174.

2. Richard P. Bagozzi, "Marketing Management: Strategies, Tactics, New Horizons," in *The Executive Course: Eleven Business Experts Tell the Corporate Leaders of Tomorrow What They Need to Know Today*, ed. Gayton E. Germane (Reading, Mass.: Addison-Wesley, 1987), 53.

3. Bagozzi, "Marketing Management."

PEST, SWOT, and the Crafts Company

PEST AND SWOT analyses can be used to help executives make decisions. SWOT is an acronym for Strengths, Weaknesses, Opportunities, and Threats, and this analysis works well for strategic planning, evaluating competitors, product and business development, and reports such as marketing communications plans. However, before a SWOT Analysis is done, it may be beneficial to first do a PEST Analysis, which considers external factors.

PEST is an acronym for Political, Economic, Social, and Technological issues that may affect a business. Sometimes PEST is extended to seven factors by adding Ecological, Legislative, and Industry Analysis; it is then known as PESTELI. However, these additional factors can be covered in the previous four factors. For instance, Ecological factors can be included under any of the four PEST headings, Legislative factors can be included in the Political factors, and Industry Analysis factors can be included in the Economic factors. Table 7.1 shows some of the external factors that may have an impact on a business. In looking at those factors, it is easy to understand why a business should consider the external environment before it begins the marketing process.

Based on the factors that a business addresses in its PEST Analysis, it can perform a SWOT Analysis more easily. Remember: a PEST Analysis measures a market while a SWOT Analysis measures a business, product, service, proposition, or idea.

Table 7.2 shows the numerous factors to consider in a SWOT Analysis. Each business has to identify the factors that are relevant for its analysis. The first two categories, Strengths and Weaknesses, are internal—factors that can be found within the business or company. The next two categories, Opportunities and Threats, are external—factors that can be found outside the business or company. The PEST Analysis should help for the second two.[1]

TABLE 7.1
PEST Analysis

POLITICAL FACTORS	ECONOMIC FACTORS
Ecological and environmental regulation	Economic growth (overall)
Taxation legislation (corporate)	Economic growth (by industry sector)
Taxation legislation (consumer)	Overseas economies and trends
Trade restrictions and tariffs	Taxation issues (impact on consumer disposable income; incentives to invest in capital equipment)
European and international trade regulation	
Consumer protection	
Employment laws	
Government organization and attitude	
Government term and change	Government spending (overall and specific)
Competitive regulation	Taxation specific to products and services
Funding, grants, and initiatives	Seasonality and weather issues
Home market lobbying and pressure groups	Market and trade cycles
International pressure groups	Market routes and distribution trends
Risk of military invasion	Customer and end-user drivers
	Interest and exchange rates (effects by overseas on demand customers; effect on cost of imported components)
	Inflation rates
	Labor costs (minimum wage, unemployment benefits)
	Stage of the business cycle
SOCIAL FACTORS	**TECHNOLOGICAL FACTORS**
Lifestyle trends	Industry technology development
Demographics (age structure of the population; gender; family size and composition; changing nature of occupations)	Research funding by the government
	Research funding by industry
	Energy use and costs
Consumer attitudes and opinions	Associated and dependent technologies
Income distribution (disposable income)	
Media views	Replacement technology and solutions
Education	
Law changes affecting social factors	Maturity of technology
Brand, company, technology image	Manufacturing maturity and capacity
Consumer buying patterns	Information and communications
Fashion and role models	Consumer buying mechanisms and technology
Health and welfare	
Major events and influences	Technology legislation
Buying access and trends	Innovation potential
Ethnic and religious factors	Technology access, licensing, patents
Living conditions	
Advertising and publicity	Intellectual property issues
Population growth rate	

TABLE 7.2
SWOT Analysis

STRENGTHS	WEAKNESSES
Advantages of the company	Disadvantages of the company
Advantages of the product/service	Disadvantages of the product/service
Capabilities of the company	Gaps in capabilities of the company
Competitive advantages	Lack of competitive advantages
Unique selling points	Reputation, presence, and reach
Resources, assets, and employees	Financial problems
Experience and knowledge of employees and company	Own known vulnerabilities
Financial reserves, likely returns	Deadlines and pressures
Marketing (awareness, reach, distribution)	Cash flow, start-up cash-drain
Innovative aspects	Continuity, supply chain robustness
Location	Reliability of data, plan predictability
Price, value, quality	Morale, commitment, leadership
Accreditations, qualifications, certifications	Accreditations
Management	Processes and systems
Cultural, attitudinal, behavioral	
OPPORTUNITIES	**THREATS**
Market developments	Political effects
Competitors' vulnerabilities	Legislative effects
Industry or lifestyle trends	Environmental effects
Technology development and innovation	Competitor intentions
Global influences	Market demand
New markets, vertical, horizontal	New technologies, services, ideas
Niche target markets	Vital contracts and partners
Geographical, export, import	Sustaining internal capabilities
New unique selling propositions	Obstacles
Tactics	Insurmountable weaknesses
Business and product development	Loss of key staff
Information and research	Sustainable financial backing
Partnerships, agencies, distribution	Economy (home and abroad)
Seasonal, weather, fashion influences	Seasonal weather effects

THE CASE

Lee Thompson has worked at the Crafts Company for 10 years. Starting as a researcher in the marketing department, she was promoted within a year primarily because of her work ethic. She was promoted to vice president of marketing just last year.

Seated at her desk, Lee was looking at several reports that related to the company's newest product, which had not been released to the U.S. market. The product, a powered jigsaw that could be operated with one hand, was designed for those who enjoyed woodworking at home. Unfortunately, the product had problems. During testing, the blade had a tendency to break after 15 minutes of continuous use. The metal used to make the blade was inferior compared to the metal used to make the blade in the leading brand. It was not Cobalt steel, which some manufacturers, including the maker of the leading brand, used. However, the leading brand's product, which was similar in appearance, was not as light. It was slightly larger, too.

Personnel in Research and Development had assured Lee that the metal used to make the blade would be coming from a different supplier, before the product would be released to the market. They assured her that the metal from the different supplier was Cobalt steel. Still, Lee wondered if the product's overall design was the cause for the blade to break. She had examined the product and had noticed that perhaps too much pressure was put on the blade when the product was used as intended. But she did not use saws and other tools, so she could only go by what others had told her.

Lee looked at the advertising budget that had been approved; she had $750,000. This amount, she realized, would be enough to introduce the product during the first year. The ads would appear in woodworking magazines, and brochures about the product would be given to managers at stores such as Wal-Mart and Home Depot. The Crafts Company was financially secure, and its upper management strongly believed in advertising its products. Based on sales, some of the company's products were in second and third place behind the best-selling brands.

Lee also examined a report on suppliers, which included the suppliers of the plastic that was used in almost every product the company manufactured. She noticed that prices had been steadily increasing, especially during the past year. Problems in other parts of the world were causing instability in prices for such specific goods as oil. And the price of oil affects the price of plastics.

Another report concerned an electric drill that had been one of the company's best-selling products. Unfortunately, the company had to recall the product earlier that year because of a possible short in the electrical cord. Lee remembered the recall well; she had helped diffuse the potential public relations nightmare for the Crafts Company by issuing a statement that went to retailers, newspapers, magazines, television stations, and other media, informing the public about the possible problem and recall. Consumers had the choice of either exchanging their drills for new ones or having their products repaired at no charge.

After reading the reports, Lee turned to a trade magazine that was popular among those who worked in the crafts and tools industry. She was about to put it aside when she noticed an article about a new portable jigsaw that was about to enter the U.S. market. Lee looked at the accompanying photograph. The product was very similar in appearance to the jigsaw that the Crafts Company had designed. She read the article and learned that the product weighed almost the same as the Crafts Company's, and it could be operated with one hand. The product was manufactured by the Crafts Company's closest competitor, Bosch, which was as financially sound as the Crafts Company but stronger than Crafts in international markets.

Lee wondered if the president of Crafts had read the article. She decided to find out.

QUESTIONS

1. Do you think the president of the company will decide to cancel the introduction of the new jigsaw when he learns about the Bosch product that is about to enter the U.S. market? Why? Why not?
2. Let's say the Crafts Company releases the product in the U.S. market. Based on the information in the case, develop a SWOT Analysis that will help Lee Thompson prepare a marketing plan for the product.
3. Do you think the Crafts Company has problems with its suppliers? Why? Why not?
4. Do you think $750,000 is enough for the advertising campaign that will introduce the jigsaw in the United States? Why? Why not?
5. Based on your SWOT Analysis, do you think the product can be successful in the U.S. market? Why? Why not?
6. If Bosch releases its jigsaw before the Crafts Company releases its product, do you think the Crafts Company's product will be able to compete? Why? Why not?
7. Considering that another product had to be recalled, do you think the Crafts Company may have problems in manufacturing products? If so, what are the problems and what do you think the company should do to resolve these problems? Explain.
8. Do you think Lee has enough information to prepare a marketing plan for the product? Why? Why not?

NOTE

1. Much of the information on PEST and SWOT analyses, including data in tables 7.1 and 7.2, is adapted from the following: "PEST Market Analysis Tool" by Alan Chapman (www.businessballs.com), 2004; "SWOT Analysis" by Alan Chapman (www.businessballs.com), 2004; "SWOT Analysis for Creative, Service and Professional Firms" (www.adcracker.com), 2004; "Startups: SWOT Analysis" (www.startups.co.uk), 2004; "SWOT Analysis: Lesson" (www.marketingteacher.com), 2004; "SWOT Analysis" (www.quickmba.com), 2004; "SWOT Analysis" by James Manktelow (www.mindtools.com), 2004; "Using SWOT Data" (www.startups.co.uk), 2004; "Strengths—Weaknesses—Opportunities—Threats (SWOT) Analysis for Start-Up Ventures" (www.1000ventures.com), 2004; "What Is PEST Analysis?" (www.marketingteacher.com), 2004; "PEST Analysis" (www.netmba.com), 2004; "Strategy—Introduction to PEST Analysis" (www.tutor2u.net), 2004; and "Strategy—SWOT Analysis" (www.tutor2u.net), 2004.

PART II

The Consumer

McNair & Company
Effective Positioning and the Smart Creative Brief

AS THE REGIONAL Airlines commuter flight gained speed, Will Jackson felt both a sense of relief and a little dread. Relief because his two-day "total immersion" in the business and marketing needs of Atlas Industries was over. Dread because now he would have to translate more than 12 hours of formal meeting notes, and numerous informal conversations, into a "picture" that could be used to restore Atlas's profitability. After so many meetings, PowerPoint presentations, personal interviews, a plant tour, and a bit of gossip and rumor, Will wondered where to start.

ATLAS INDUSTRIES

Atlas's core product is batteries—not the kind you put into flashlights, but batteries for lawn tractors, golf carts, go-karts, and motorcycles. A uniqueness of the Atlas product line is the many sizes and shapes that are produced. This allows many original equipment manufacturers (OEMs) to spec Atlas batteries for the products they manufacture. By all indications, Atlas batteries are durable, last beyond their warranty periods, and have few returns. They are equal in power output to the competitors' products, but generally lighter and safer to handle.

While there is a range of pricing for various models, generally the price is $35–75 at retail for a battery warranted for 48 months. Most competitors only warrant their batteries in this price range for 36 months. Distributors mark the batteries up 30 percent, and the majority have been pleased with the product's performance, lack of returns, prompt delivery by Atlas, and the product's quality reputation. Several Asian battery manufacturers have been offering to sell Atlas distributors "equivalent" batteries at a price that would allow distributors to mark them up 50 percent to retailers.

Within 120 days, Atlas's newest innovation, a "lifetime battery," would be ready to ship to distributors. Using a revolutionary new technology, these batteries promised to perform almost indefinitely with standard maintenance, and certainly beyond the longest-lasting competitive battery now on the market, which claimed a 75-month life.

Atlas expected to offer this new battery at only a 25 percent retail price premium over its best batteries now being sold. The 75-month battery being sold by a competitor retailed for somewhere between $100 and $115.

WILL JACKSON

As the newest member of Fran Franzini's account team at McNair & Company, Will was selected to visit Atlas Industries with Fran because of his recent experience working on a similar account at a smaller ad agency. There, he had a hands-on relationship with one of Atlas's primary competitors when that agency created a multimedia campaign that included TV ads, four-color trade magazine ads, a direct mail campaign to distributors, an e-commerce portal, and numerous other collateral pieces that were used throughout the campaign. Just like Atlas Industries, Will's former client sold mostly to distributors, but also directly to a list of "house account" retailers.

Yet, while their clients were similar, the two ad agencies couldn't be more different. Bright Idea! Advertising was a relatively small, "boutique" agency that prided itself on award-winning creative strategies. The average age of the staff was 24, and that included the president and creative director, both of whom shared a talent and passion for dramatic, breakthrough creative solutions. Because they were such a small group, decisions were generally made based on "instinct," and often the entire staff of 12 participated in creating ad campaigns over pizza and beer. And, while there had been suggestions that a more formalized process be put in place, the agency's success and continuing creative awards told the owners that they were doing just fine with the system they had.

Will had always loved these late-night creative sessions, where ideas flowed pro and con, where individuals made on-the-spot sketches of executional elements, often while others were still talking. The backdrop for these idea sessions was a commitment on the part of all participants that *no idea*, no matter how off-key or ridiculous it seemed at first, was to be discarded without discussion. Often, ideas would begin to flow by someone first shouting, "Hey, how about this?" or "I've got an idea!" or "What if . . . ?" One of the other "rules" was that, if at all possible, *original* ideas were sought. The quickest way to get overshouted or "dissed" was to propose an idea "that had already been done." It was this culture that led the agency to offer quirky, edgy, and offbeat ad campaigns.

The decision to leave Bright Idea! was Will's, brought on in part by his desire to work at a bigger ad agency, make more money, and grow professionally. Bright Idea!, for all its energy and creativity, was a business run like a "fun house." Documentation was scarce, expense control was lacking, and clients were viewed as stepping-stones to greatness for the agency. This creative chaos, while fun and freewheeling, had its career-limiting boundaries, and Will sensed it was time to leave. This is when he contacted McNair & Company, one of the largest advertising agencies in Chicago.

Now, however, he wondered if he had done the right thing. Atlas Industries was a large client that was in trouble. Time was running out, or at least that is what Will perceived. To a person, the marketing and advertising management at Atlas were impatient for a campaign that would increase sales, gain market share, and lead to financial stability. They talked about all the tools that Will was familiar with—ads, brochures, Internet, P-O-P, dealer kits, and incentives—but clearly they were looking for a creative "home run" to get things back on track.

As the plane climbed through 10,000 feet and Fran decided to take a nap, Will took out his notebook and looked for a place to start. First, he made a list of key facts he had gathered:

- Atlas sales were off 7 percent compared to the same time last year. Last year was the worst in the company's 23-year history.
- Many of Atlas's best salespeople were shell-shocked or looking for another job.
- Two new Asian competitors were aggressively targeting Atlas distributors with competitive products that were of higher quality with competitive pricing.
- Atlas's manufacturing plants were running at only 60 percent of capacity, with manufacturing costs and prompt delivery times being compromised.
- Distributors, used to getting sales promotion support and retail advertising to "pull" Atlas's products through to retail, were nervous about Atlas's financial situation.
- Rumors were flying that Atlas was for sale or seeking an alliance with a competitor.

Yet, in Atlas's favor were the following:

- All of Atlas's patents were in place, and quality had not been affected in the manufacturing slowdown.
- The Atlas brand was still seen as representing innovation, quality, and integrity.
- All Atlas products were manufactured in the United States.
- Sales support for Atlas distributors was still among the best in the category.
- Product Development had just finished successfully field-testing a revolutionary improvement in Atlas's core product, and it would be ready for introduction within 120 days.
- The ownership of Atlas had just committed $1.2 million "to get the word out" (whatever that meant).

As Will organized his thoughts, he started to feel more confident about an idea he had been turning over in his head even before the trip to Atlas. And the more he thought about the idea, the better he liked it. No, the more he thought about it, the better he *loved* it! Surely, this would make both his former agency and McNair sit up and take notice of both Atlas and Will. As Will began to sketch out his ideas, he felt on fire creatively. Ads, collateral, e-commerce, and all of the needs that were discussed over the past two days now seemed like no-brainers. It was easy once you had a great idea! He couldn't wait to show Fran what needed to be done, and he would, just as soon as she awoke.

In his exuberance, however, Will had forgotten a key bit of process that made his new agency different from Bright Idea! At McNair & Company, particularly for major campaigns, account executives were expected to write a "creative brief." This single sheet, or at most two-page document, was the starting point for the input of information and insight to McNair's creative department. The brief had to be well written, and it had to capture the most important needs and nuances of the client's business situation. At McNair, the creative process was not the free-for-all that it was at Bright Idea! At McNair, the owners prided themselves on problem-solving creative strategies targeted to all of the important audiences that make any new campaign successful.

As the pilot turned on the Fasten Seat Belt sign and got ready to land, Fran awoke. Will could hardly contain his enthusiasm and pride as he began to bombard Fran with creative ideas and executions that would be *perfect* for Atlas. A new theme line. TV commercial ideas. Print ads. Man, this stuff was great! He couldn't *wait* to get back to the agency tomorrow and share his solutions with anyone who would listen.

As he blurted out idea after idea, Fran asked to see his creative brief. Caught somewhat off guard, he said, "What? Oh, I'll do that tomorrow."

"How can we possibly position Atlas, amid the problems it is having, with a new product line set to roll out in 120 days, without solid information?" asked Fran. "How can we reach both the distributors and the end-user with what I think might be an entirely different message? One campaign, no matter how great an idea, won't work. I love your enthusiasm, and your 'get it done' spirit, but it all needs to start with a creative brief. Actually, we probably need *two* different briefs, one for the distributors and one for the end-users. That's where we need to start."

Fran gave Will a copy of the creative brief format McNair used. "Here, think about this tonight. We can go over it in the morning."

QUESTIONS

1. Do you think an orderly creative process will yield creative answers that are as good as those generated by brainstorming?
2. Is "creativity" in a person innate, or can anyone learn it?
3. What is meant by the term "positioning"?
4. Is a creative brief a limiting document, as some creative people charge?
5. How can a creative brief be used with a client?

6. See figure 8.1 for a creative brief used by Locomotion Creative in Nashville, Tennessee. There are many creative brief formats in use by agencies and design firms, both large and small. The important thing is that they give useful and insightful information to the creative team to "frame the opportunity." Download the pdf of this form from the book's page on www.rowmanlittlefield.com and complete it based on the facts, and your interpretation of those facts, from Will and Fran's visit to Atlas Industries. Remember, Fran wanted Will to do two creative briefs.

CREATIVE STRATEGY

TARGET AUDIENCE
Who the advertising is aimed at and all demographic and/or psychographic data pertinent to this job.

SOURCE OF BUSINESS
What products or services are now being used by the target? Do we intend to replace them? With whom are we competing?

ADVERTISING OBJECTIVE
A focused problem-solving statement of what the advertising should accomplish. General Trail? Create or change image? Introduce new product or new features? Create interest via a promotion?

PRIMARY RATIONAL BENEFIT
Single-minded statement of the functional performance we are promising our target. This is the rational statement, not the emotional statement.

SUPPORT
The reason why. The permission to believe our Primary Rational Benefit. Must be focused and deliverable.

EMOTIONAL APPEAL
What the Primary Rational Benefit means to our target from an emotional standpoint. How do we want to impact our target's "state off heart"?

TONALITY
Tone or "personality" we want to establish or reinforce. What image do we want our target to take away?

MANDATORIES
Any legal/client dictates or other required elements that must be addressed.

FIGURE 8.1

Consumer Buying Behavior and the Plumber Clothing Company

TYPICALLY, CONSUMERS go through several stages from the time they first consider buying a product or service until after their purchase:

1. Awareness of a need (problem).
2. Activity to determine how to satisfy the need (information search).
3. Decision to buy (evaluation of alternatives).
4. Act of buying (purchase).
5. Feelings after purchase (post-purchase behavior).

For a convenience item, such as a soft drink, the awareness of a need, activity to determine how to satisfy the need, and the decision to buy will be almost simultaneous. For a shopping good, the awareness of a need and the activity to determine how to satisfy the need may be a very long-term process.

DECISION FACTORS

Various factors influence one's decision to buy. These factors can be personal, psychological, social, or cultural.

Personal factors include one's physical age or the stage of the life cycle one happens to be in. Younger people tend to buy more than older people, for instance, because older people generally have most of what they need. Also, many older people have limited incomes. Another personal factor is occupation and consequently financial situation; one's income has to be considered, especially if the product is expensive. Lifestyle is a factor: some people are conservative in their purchases and some are extravagant.

Another factor is one's personality and consequently self-concept; one may think that a product will enhance one's self-image, for instance.

Psychological factors include a person's motivation as a result of needs. Another is learning based on experience of buying products and services. Another is one's perception based on stimuli (information gained from ads, promotions, articles, and programs about a product). Other factors are one's beliefs or opinions and attitudes about a product as a result of learning about it and purchasing it (experience).

Social factors include various reference groups. Personal groups, for example, are family and friends. Membership groups include clubs or organizations, schools, colleges, and places of religious worship. Opinion leaders or experts are professionals or other people you trust. Any of these groups may have one or more members who will share information about a product, especially when asked. Aspirational groups are groups one feels positive about or aspires to belong to, while dissociative groups are groups one feels negative about or rejects.

Cultural factors include one's nationality, religion, ethnicity, and geographic region or location. Related to these is the social class one is a part of. Social classes include the following:

Upper uppers—about 1 percent of the population. These individuals are members of the highest economic class and generally have the most inherited wealth.

Lower uppers—about 2 percent of the population. These individuals are professionals who are successful, financially speaking. They may be considered the nouveau riche.

Upper middles—about 12 percent of the population. These individuals are white-collar professionals who manage corporations or own small businesses and earn a comfortable living.

Middle class—about 32 percent of the population. These individuals work for a living and live in good neighborhoods. They tend to persuade their children to get a college education.

Working class—about 38 percent of the population. These individuals are typically blue-collar employees who depend on relatives for economic and emotional support.

Upper lowers—about 9 percent of the population. These individuals work in unskilled jobs; consequently, their income provides a standard of living that borders on poverty.

Lower lowers—about 7 percent of the population. These individuals are usually unemployed and are on welfare.[1]

Members of the various social classes take different approaches in life. As a result, advertisers must differ, too, especially with regard to the media they use and their advertising content. Regarding the latter, advertisers must provide content that prospective consumers can identify and relate to. Advertisers need to make certain that they do not violate the norms (rules or standards) of the group to which the prospective consumers belong.

MINORITY GROUP MARKETS

The following large minority groups, which can be considered markets by advertisers, are found in the United States and are based primarily on ethnicity.

The African American Market

There are almost 35 million African Americans, for slightly more than 12 percent of the country's population. This group has a purchasing power of more than $570 billion. In the past, African American households spent more on apparel, telephone services, and natural gas than other American households. They also spent a higher proportion of their after-tax income on housing, electricity, transportation, and food consumed at home. The majority of African American families rent apartments or houses. African Americans are becoming more conscious about education, though fewer than 15 percent have a college degree.[2]

The Asian American Market

There are more than 10 million Asian Americans, for almost 4 percent of the country's population. This group has a purchasing power of more than $250 billion. In fact, this group's purchasing power has grown faster than that of any other group in the United States. The primary reason for this is that Asian Americans are better educated than the average American; almost 45 percent have a college education. Consequently, a large proportion of them hold top-level jobs in management or professional specialties.[3]

The Hispanic American Market

There are more than 35 million Hispanic Americans, for more than 12 percent of the country's population. This group is now the largest minority group in the United States. Although Hispanic Americans can be found across the country, about 2 million reside in New York City. Other large Hispanic communities can be found in California, Florida, Illinois, and Texas. Overall, this group has a purchasing power of more than $425 billion, and their purchasing power has grown faster than that of the African American group.

Hispanic Americans earn less than other groups, but they spend more on food consumed at home, telephone services, and apparel. They also spend a higher proportion of their after-tax income on housing, personal care products, and services. However, they spend less on reading material, education, tobacco, health care, and entertainment. The majority of Hispanic households rent apartments or houses.[4]

The Native American Market

There are more than 2 million Native Americans in the United States, for almost 1 percent of the country's population. Most American Indians live on reservations, where most of their business and leisure activity occurs. Native American groups do not fare as well as other minority groups, economically speaking, although certain subgroups have seen improvement.[5]

THE CASE

T. J. Plumber arrived in the United States from England and in 1930 founded the Plumber Clothing Company, in Ft. Worth, Texas. Today, the company produces dress slacks, casual slacks, sport coats, and shirts for men. Its products are produced in Canada, the Dominican Republic, and Mexico, among other countries, and they are sold primarily in North America and Europe.

The company was privately owned by members of the Plumber family until 1990, when it went public. The same year the company introduced wrinkle-free pants for men. Later, it introduced a casual line of clothing for men in response to the casual-dress revolution that eventually caught on in offices in the United States and other countries. In 2000 the company launched an expandable waistband line of pants in response to men's ever increasing waistlines. A year later it launched a stainless line of pants and shirts for men.

Recently the company introduced a men's line of casual and dress clothing that would not fade, shrink, stain, or wrinkle. Using the campaign theme "Time Has Come Today," the line was advertised initially in magazines such as *CARGO*, *GQ*, and *Sports Illustrated*, as well as on ABC, NBC, CBS, ESPN, and Fox television networks. Commercials appeared during NFL programs and during college football games. Commercials were broadcast on radio, too. A typical magazine advertisement contained a model dressed in the clothing (shirt and pants); the model was standing and facing toward the right. The headline—"Time Has Come Today"—was positioned above the four-color photograph. Body copy discussing the features and benefits of the line of clothing was positioned below the photograph, above the company's logo. The typical television commercial featured one or more models moving in a work or social environment; a voiceover discussed the line of clothing's features and benefits. An original piece of music opened and ended the spot. The typical radio commercial was similar in that a voiceover discussed the features and benefits of the line of clothing; music opened and ended it.

Now Steven Markham, Plumber's vice president of marketing, wants to know if the "Time Has Come Today" advertising campaign attracted the intended target market—males age 35 to 55—and if the initial advertising campaign needs to be changed in order to persuade the target market to buy more of the line. He also wants to know if additional target markets should be considered and how these markets should be reached—that is, what message should be communicated in the advertising and which media should be used.

QUESTIONS

1. Based on the descriptions above, do you think the initial advertising campaign attracted the intended target market? If yes, what specifically did you find appropriate, relevant, or appealing about the initial advertising campaign (advertising message) that caused consumers to buy? If no, what specifically do you think needs to be changed to cause consumers to buy?

2. Explain how the initial advertising campaign (advertising message) needs to be changed to persuade more of the target market to buy more of the line.

3. Based on the information provided, do you think males age 35 to 55 should be the only intended target market? If yes, why? If no, why not?

4. If you answered no to the above, identify the additional target markets and explain why they should be considered.

5. Explain how the additional target markets will impact the advertising message and media chosen.

6. If the company learns that minority group members are not buying much of the line because of the advertising, what do you think Markham needs to do? Explain. If you suggest that he needs a new advertising campaign, present ideas for one. Then discuss the media needed for your campaign to be successful. Finally, explain how your campaign will affect the target market (to make consumers aware of the products, to make them desire the products, to make them buy the products, etc.).

7. If the company learns that minority group members are not buying much of the line because of product characteristics or price, what do you think Markham needs to do? Explain.

NOTES

1. Adapted from Richard P. Coleman and Lee P. Rainwater, *Social Standing in America: New Dimension of Class* (New York: Basic Books, 1978).

2. Jeffrey M. Humphreys, "African-American Buying Power by Place of Residence: 1990–1999," www.selig.uga.edu/forecast/totalbuy/afr-amer. Also, "DP-1. Profile of General Demographic Characteristics: 2000," U.S. Census Bureau.

3. Jeffrey M. Humphreys, "Asian-American Buying Power by Place of Residence: 1990–1999," *Georgia Business and Economic Conditions* 59, no. 1 (January–February 1999): 1–7. Also, "DP-1. Profile of General Demographic Characteristics: 2000," U.S. Census Bureau.

4. Jeffrey M. Humphreys, "Hispanic Buying Power by Place of Residence: 1990–1999," *Georgia Business and Economic Conditions* 58, no. 6 (November–December 1998): 1–8. Also, Alison Stein Wellner, "The Census Report," *American Demographics* 24, no. 1 (January 2002): S5. Also, "DP-1. Profile of General Demographic Characteristics: 2000," U.S. Census Bureau.

5. "DP-1. Profile of General Demographic Characteristics: 2000," U.S. Census Bureau.

Segmenting, Targeting, Positioning (STP) and Here's to Your Health Frozen Dinners

MARKET SEGMENTATION is the process of dividing a large heterogeneous market into submarkets, or segments, that are more similar or homogeneous in terms of their characteristics as well as needs or desires. The submarket or segment that a company identifies for its product is called a target market. For a submarket or segment to be useful in marketing, it must be measurable, it must be large enough so that sales from it will generate profits, it must be reachable, it must be responsive to the marketing program, and it must be stable—that is, the group's needs and wants must not change anytime soon.[1]

There are several bases on which prospective consumers are segmented. These include demographics, psychographics, geographics, geodemographics, product usage, and benefits, among others.

DEMOGRAPHIC SEGMENTATION

Demographics include age, education, ethnicity, family size, income, gender, occupation, and religion, among other factors.

Age and Family Composition

According to the 2000 U.S. census, more than 280 million individuals live in the United States. Table 10.1 shows a breakdown of the U.S. population by age category based on the 2000 census. The same data indicate that the average household size is 2.59 individuals. The average family size is 3.14 individuals. See table 10.2.

TABLE 10.1
U.S. Population by Age, 2000

AGE	NUMBER OF PERSONS	PERCENTAGE OF POPULATION
Under 5 years	19,175,798	6.8
5 to 9 years	20,549,505	7.3
10 to 14 years	20,528,072	7.3
15 to 19 years	20,219,890	7.2
20 to 24 years	18,964,001	6.7
25 to 34 years	39,891,724	14.2
35 to 44 years	45,148,527	16.0
45 to 54 years	37,677,952	13.4
55 to 59 years	13,469,237	4.8
60 to 64 years	10,805,447	3.8
65 to 74 years	18,390,986	6.5
75 to 84 years	12,361,180	4.4
85 years and over	4,239,587	1.5
Median age: 35.3 years		

Source: U.S. Census Bureau.

TABLE 10.2
Family Households in the United States, 2000

HOUSEHOLDS BY TYPE	NUMBER	PERCENTAGE
Family households (families)	71,787,347	68.1
With own children under 18	34,588,366	32.8
Married-only family	54,493,232	51.7
With own children under 18	24,835,505	23.5
Female householder, no husband present	12,900,103	12.2
With own children under 18	7,561,874	7.2
Nonfamily households	33,692,754	31.9
Householder living alone	27,672,706	25.8
Householder 65 years and over	9,722,857	9.2
Households with individuals under 18	38,022,115	36.0
Households with individuals 65 years and over	24,672,706	23.4

Average household size: 2.59 persons
Average family size: 3.14 persons

Source: U.S. Census Bureau.

As table 10.2 shows, there are more than 71 million family households in the United States, totaling more than 68 percent of the total households in the country. Married couples head more than 54 million, or 51.7 percent, of these family households, while almost 13 million, or 12.2 percent, are headed by a female only.

More than 38 million households, or 36 percent, include individuals under 18 years of age, while more than 24 million households, or 23.4 percent, include individuals 65 and over.

Income and Benefits for All Households

More than 10 million U.S. households earn less than $10,000 a year, while more than 20 million households earn between $50,000 and $75,000. More than 27 million households earn between $15,000 and $35,000. The median household income is $41,349, while the mean household income is $55,263.[2]

Demographic factors are not usually enough for a company to identify a market. Psychographic factors are also considered.

PSYCHOGRAPHIC SEGMENTATION

Generally, psychographic factors include consumers' activities, interests, and opinions (AIO), and these AIO items are used to construct a consumer psychographic profile. Usually marketing research firms are hired by clients to conduct psychographic studies that have been tailored to the client's product categories. However, several firms have developed psychographic profiles of individuals that are not necessarily related to any product or service category.

For instance, the Stanford Research Institute Consulting Business Intelligence, or SRI, developed the Values and Lifestyles Psychographic Segmentation system, or VALS. VALS typology indicates that consumer behavior is motivated by three self-orientations: principle, status, and action. According to SRI, "Principle-oriented consumers are guided in their choices by abstract, idealized criteria, rather than by feelings, events, or desire for approval and opinions of others. Status-oriented consumers look for products and services that demonstrate success to their peers. Action-oriented consumers are guided by a desire for social or physical activity, variety, and risk taking."[3]

VALS also segments by resources, which refer to psychological, physical, demographic, and material means that are available to consumers. The resources continuum (minimal at the bottom to abundant at the top) encompasses education, income, self-confidence, health, eagerness to buy, intelligence, and energy level. VALS identifies eight segments: actualizers, fulfilleds, believers, achievers, strivers, experiencers, makers, and strugglers.[4]

Another system, MONITOR MindBase, was developed by Yankelovich Partners. The system helps clients target specific consumers. In the MONITOR MindBase, eight major groups of consumers have been identified by their attitudes and motivations: up and comers, aspiring achievers, realists, new traditionalists, family centereds, individualists, renaissance masters, and maintainers. These major consumer groups have been separated into 32 distinct segments. Some have more segments than others.[5]

GEODEMOGRAPHIC SEGMENTATION

Geodemographic, a conjunction of geography and demography or demographic, is based on the notion that people who live in similar neighborhoods or even postal ZIP-code zones are inclined to have similar demographics, attitudes, interests, and opinions. In short, they will have similar lifestyles and consumption patterns.

Several marketing research firms have developed geodemographic market clusters for the country's 250,000-plus neighborhoods. Specifically, these clusters represent people who have similar demographics and lifestyles. For instance, in the early 1970s Claritas created PRIZM (Potential Rating Index by ZIP Markets), one of the most widely used lifestyle segmentation systems in the United States. PRIZM applies the adage "Birds of a feather flock together" by assigning every neighborhood in the country to one of 66 clusters. Each cluster describes the demographics and lifestyles of the people living in that neighborhood.[6]

THE CASE

Here's to Your Health Foods, based in Minneapolis, Minnesota, is one of the newest packaged food companies in the United States. It offers a variety of brands that can be found in grocery stores and other retail outlets, as well as in restaurant and food-service establishments. One of its best-selling brands is the Here's to Your Health line of frozen dinners, which was the idea of George Fogel, the chief executive officer. Fogel studied Americans' eating habits for years and realized that their diet was not very good. Fogel, who had seen his mother and father gain considerable weight and later develop heart disease, tried to find frozen meals that were tasty and nutritious; however, most frozen dinners were not very healthy. So Fogel realized that there was a need for meals that offered good taste and nutrition.

In 2000 Here's to Your Health introduced five frozen dinners that were low in fat, sodium, and cholesterol. After some persuasion, grocery store managers began carrying the dinners. Then, sales of the dinners caused the managers to take notice. The brand was desired by those who wished to eat a low-fat, nutritious meal. Retailers who had been reluctant to carry the brand now insisted on having it for their customers.

Although men eat frozen dinners more often than women, the Here's to Your Health line of frozen dinners was aimed primarily at women age 30 and older. However, the company soon learned that men also liked the Here's to Your Health dinners. The brand was popular among men and women age 40 and older. It was only natural for the company to expand the product line based on the brand's popularity. Today, Here's to Your Health offers more than 50 products—from frozen dinners to frozen desserts. Of course, the company's competition did not stand still. Indeed, several companies expanded their product lines as well. They also focused on health in their advertising, much like Here's to Your Health.

Graham Hart worked for Carolyn Matson, the vice president of marketing in charge of the Here's to Your Health line of frozen dinners. Graham read the following section of a report that researchers had provided:

> Researchers have found that adolescents in the United States are overweight. In one study, 12.6 percent of boys aged 13 were heavy, while 10.8 percent of girls aged 13 were heavy. Among 15-year-old boys 13.9 percent were overweight, while among 15-year-old girls 15.1 percent were overweight.
>
> According to a press release by the U.S. Department of Health and Human Services, 300,000 deaths a year are associated with obesity and overweight. Obesity among adults has doubled since 1980, while overweight among adolescents has tripled. Only 3 percent of all Americans meet at least four of the five federal Food Guide Pyramid recommendations for the intake of grains, fruits, vegetables, dairy products, and meats. Less than one-third of Americans meet the federal recommendations to engage in at least 30 minutes of moderate physical activity at least five days a week, while 40 percent of adults engage in no leisure-time physical activity at all.
>
> In women, overweight and obesity are higher among members of racial and ethnic minority populations than in non-Hispanic white women. In men, Mexican Americans have a higher prevalence of overweight and obesity than non-Hispanic men, while non-Hispanic white men have a greater prevalence than non-Hispanic black men.

Table 10.3 shows the percentage of adults who were overweight and obese in the early 2000s.[7]

Graham considered what he had read. He thought about the new line of frozen dinners that the company was about to introduce. Each of the five dinners contained bigger portions and was nutritious. Each dinner had low levels of fat, sodium, and cholesterol. In fact, each dinner was 98 percent fat-free and had between 325 and 425 calories. Each dinner contained steak, chicken, or pasta and two side items, such as vegetables.

Graham had 10 days to prepare a presentation for Carolyn in which he would identify and describe the most appropriate target market for the new line of frozen dinners.

TABLE 10.3
Overweight and Obese U.S. Adults (by sex)

CHARACTERISTIC	MALES		FEMALES	
	OVERWEIGHT	OBESE	OVERWEIGHT	OBESE
All ages	66.5	22.6	49.9	22.3
18 to 24 years	45.1	14.0	32.2	13.7
25 to 44 years	69.0	23.2	47.4	21.6
45 to 64 years	73.8	27.4	58.3	27.8
65 years and over	63.7	19.2	54.5	20.7
Hispanic	71.5	21.9	61.3	26.4
White, non-Hispanic	66.7	22.4	46.1	20.0
Black, non-Hispanic	66.6	28.0	68.5	36.4
Asian/Other Pacific Islander, non-Hispanic	38.9	6.6	26.1	6.1

Source: Statistical Abstract of the United States: 2003, U.S. Census Bureau.

QUESTIONS

1. Do you think the information about segmentation provided in this chapter is enough for Graham Hart to identify a suitable target market for the new line of frozen dinners? If yes, why? If not, why not?

2. Do you think Graham has read enough information from the report to identify and describe the most appropriate target market for the new line of frozen dinners? If yes, provide a brief description of the target market. If not, what additional information do you think he needs? Where could he find this information (what sources)?

3. Do you think the information on segmentation together with the part of the report that Graham has read is enough for him to identify and describe the most appropriate target market? If yes, provide a brief description of the target market. If not, what additional information do you think he needs? Where could he find this information (what sources)?

4. If Graham had to identify a segment of the target market that would be inclined to purchase more often the new line of frozen dinners, which segment would it be? Why?

5. What segment of the target market may be less inclined to purchase the new line of frozen dinners? Why would this segment be less inclined to purchase the line?

6. Do you think Graham should use the information about overweight and obese Americans to help him identify an intended target market? How many of these Americans are in the age groups that buy Here's to Your Health frozen dinners?

7. If Graham decided that overweight and obese Americans were a likely target market, suggest one or more ideas that could be used in ads to sell the new line of frozen dinners.

NOTES

1. Charles D. Schewe and Alexander Watson Hiam, *The Portable MBA in Marketing*, 2nd ed. (New York: John Wiley and Sons, 1998), 206–8.

2. U.S. Census Bureau.

3. "The VALS Segment Profiles," SRI Consulting Business Intelligence, 333 Ravenswood Avenue, Menlo Park, California.

4. "The VALS Segment Profiles."

5. "Yankelovich MONITOR MindBase," Yankelovich Partners, 200 W. Franklin Street, Chapel Hill, N.C.

6. "PRIZM," Claritas Inc., 2001, www.claritas.com/3_claritas_products/SUB/prod_seg_prizm.htm.

7. Sources: "HRSA Research Finds U.S. Teens Most Likely to Be Overweight, Immigrant Teens Face Social Problems," HRSA News Brief, U.S. Department of Health and Human Services, January 6, 2004 (http://newsroom.hrsa.gov/NewsBriefs/2004/teens.htm); "Overweight and Obesity Threaten U.S. Health Gains: Communities Can Help Address the Problem, Surgeon General Says," HHS News, U.S. Department of Health and Human Services, December 13, 2001 (www.hhs.gov/news); and *Statistical Abstract of the United States: 2003* (U.S. Census Bureau, 2004), 140.

B-to-B Marketing and the Venus 4Y

MARKETING A PRODUCT or service to another business, industry, or organization is termed business-to-business (B-to-B) marketing. Companies that research, develop, and build products for mass consumption need parts from other companies (suppliers) in order to manufacture products that their employees have designed. For instance, a manufacturer of computers needs microchips, hard drives, screens, speakers, and other parts from suppliers.

Organizations that provide services to other businesses or organizations need items from other companies so that their services are effective or efficient. For instance, a cleaning service needs cleaning solutions, hoses, and other items from other companies.

Wholesalers and retailers purchase products from manufacturers in order to resell these products at a profit to consumers and organizations. For instance, J. C. Penny, Sears, Target, and Wal-Mart purchase goods from manufacturers to sell in their respective stores.

Government agencies at the local, state, and federal level purchase goods such as equipment, machinery, and supplies. Indeed, the U.S. federal government is one of the largest customers in the world.

Of course, there are other institutions that purchase products and services in order to operate effectively and efficiently. For instance, churches and other religious establishments, colleges, hospitals, and museums purchase various products and services from other companies.

In many instances, products for industry are more complex than products for consumers. This is one reason industries selling goods to other industries use personal selling, print (especially trade) publications, and the Internet to advertise their products.

Businesses that desire to sell to other businesses must realize that there are three types of purchases made by businesses or organizations:

Straight rebuys: routinely reordering a product or products from the same suppliers used in the past.

Modified rebuys: when a routine purchase changes in some way, the buyer considers alternatives before making a selection. Changes occur when a supplier discontinues a product, raises the price of a product, or introduces a new product for the same need.

New task buy: purchasing a big-ticket item such as new equipment or real estate. Such purchases are infrequent. Because of the investment, such purchases involve research, time, and a number of decision makers.

Businesses and organizations typically have a number of individuals who are responsible for making decisions regarding purchases. These individuals make up the buying center and include the following:

Initiators: these people recognize a need in the organization that can be filled by purchasing a product or service. Initiators may be users.

Users: these people will actually use the product or service in the organization. Users may help determine the requirements of the product.

Influencers: these people influence the buying decision, usually by helping to define the specifications for the product desired. Influencers may be technical personnel.

Buyers: these people have the power to select the suppliers and negotiate the terms of the purchase.

Gatekeepers: these people have the power to prevent information from reaching certain members of the buying center.

Generally, the average number of people involved in a buying decision ranges from three to five.

Buying decisions in businesses are influenced by the company's environmental factors, the company's organizational factors, the company's personnel factors, and the company's cultural factors.

The buying process for businesses and organizations typically includes the following stages:

1. Identifying the problem or need.
2. Identifying the product that will solve the problem or fill the need.
3. Identifying the product by its physical features or characteristics and specifications.
4. Searching for quality suppliers.
5. Requesting proposals from quality suppliers.
6. Evaluating proposals and selecting a supplier.
7. Evaluating the product's performance after purchase.[1]

THE VENUS 4Y

In 2005 Venus Motor Sales released information about the Venus 4Y, a new line of cars that the company would aim primarily to Generation Y, those born between 1980 and 1995. These young drivers have been raised on the computer and the World Wide Web and will total more than 60 million by 2010.

The 4Y line will appeal to members of this group because the cars will be innovative and stylish. In addition, Venus dealers who offer the 4Y line will have sales staffs that are knowledgeable and buyer-friendly. The dealer environment will feature stylish decor and have interactive surroundings aimed at individualizing the buying experience. Prospective customers will be invited to browse, research, and examine 4Ys by themselves, but sales staffs will be available to provide assistance.

Venus Motor Sales unveiled both a 4Y sedan and coupe. Both models are priced below $15,000. The 4Y sedan is a muscular compact with four doors that appeals to young drivers. It is powered by a 100-horsepower, 1.4-liter engine, and buyers can choose between a standard five-speed manual transmission or a four-speed automatic. The 4Y sedan offers buyers several exterior colors from which to choose. Inside, the car is visually appealing with a center console and textured treatments on the doors, dashboard, and seats. The rear seat folds down, allowing plenty of storage space in the trunk.

The 4Y sedan includes the following standard features:

Air conditioning.
Power steering, windows, door locks, and outside mirrors.
Cruise control.
Antilock brakes (ABS).
Tachometer and trip meter.
Sport front bucket seats.
Cupholder.

The 4Y coupe comes with the same engine and transmission choices as the 4Y sedan, but the 4Y coupe features large door openings. The rear seat folds down, too, allowing plenty of storage space in the trunk. The interior is similar to that of the 4Y sedan. Sport bucket seats occupy the front.

The 4Y coupe has the following standard features:

Power steering, windows, door locks, and outside mirrors.
Cruise control.
Air conditioning.
Antilock brakes (ABS).
Tachometer and trip meter.
Cupholder.

Both models allow buyers to choose from five wheel-cover designs or upgrade to alloy wheels for an additional amount. Both models come standard with a Pioneer audio system, or buyers may upgrade the system for an additional amount.

THE CASE

Eva Lentzer is a buyer in the Purchasing Department of Venus, which is responsible for procuring supplies for the 4Y models of cars. Recently the department sent specifications for the models to several tire manufacturers and received bids from three of them. One manufacturer informed Eva that it needed more time, and another manufacturer advised that it could not meet the specifications because of costs.

Eva had been studying each bid for several minutes when Phil Dupont stuck his head into her office. "Eva, are you ready for the meeting?"

Eva looked up, smiled, and replied, "Yes, I think so."

"Well, let's go. I think the others are in the conference room."

Eva and Phil walked down the carpeted hall to the conference room, where every member of the buying center was sitting at the table, waiting. As they joined the group, Phil said, "Eva, why don't you share what you have."

"Okay. I'm sure you remember that we sent proposals to five manufacturers, inviting them to bid based on our specifications. Marie Patterson, who works for one of the manufacturers, claimed they could not meet our specifications—that our specifications would cost them too much money. Charlie Watts said his company was interested in submitting a bid, but he needed another week. The other three manufacturers submitted bids based on our specifications. The first said they could provide 500,000 tires at $50 a tire, for a total of $25 million. And they could meet our delivery dates with no problems. The second said they could provide the tires at $45 a tire, for a total of $22.5 million. They also said they could meet our delivery dates. And the third said they could provide the tires at $55 dollars a tire, for a total of $27.5 million. And they could deliver the tires on time."

"Eva, what do you think about giving Charlie more time to give us an estimate?" Phil asked.

"Considering that the company he works for manufactures an excellent product, I'd say we should give him more time."

"The bid may be higher than the others," Phil said.

"Well, if it is, we can go with one of the others, say, the first company at $50 a tire."

"Why not go with the second at $45 a tire?" asked Bill Masterson, who worked in engineering.

"I'm wondering why they are so much lower than the other two," Eva said.

"They may be trying to get as much business as they possibly can, considering the problems they had with one of their brands several years ago," Bill said.

Eva nodded. "You may be right, Bill."

Phil said, "I think we should wait to see what Charlie's company's bid is before we make a decision. I also think we need to check each company's website to see if they have any recalls. We don't want to go with a company that has problems."

"Phil, we checked before we decided on these manufacturers," May Carpenter, who worked in research and development, said.

"I know, but I think we need to check again to see if any of these companies have had to recall tires since the proposals were mailed."

Bill said, "That's a good idea."

"Sounds good to me," Eva said.

The remaining members nodded.

"Well, then, I'll check on the third company," Phil said. "Bill, you check on the second. Eva, you check on the first. May, you check on Charlie's company. Okay? We'll meet again when Eva gets the bid from Charlie's company and compare what we've found out."

QUESTIONS

1. Let's say that you visit the websites of the manufacturers to determine if any have had to recall tires. Let's say that you discover one of the manufacturers had recalled tires or is recalling tires. What would you suggest that the members do about this manufacturer? Would you suggest that the manufacturer not be considered, even if the manufacturer had put in a reasonable bid? Why? Why not?

2. Let's say that none of the manufacturers have had to recall tires in the past few weeks, and that Charlie's company's bid is the same as the third company's bid, $55 a tire. What would you suggest that the members do? Eliminate both because their bids are the same? Consider both because their bids are the same? Or would you suggest something different? Explain.

3. If Charlie's company's bid is the same as the third company's—that is, more costly than the other two companies' bids—what would you suggest that the members decide? Explain your reasoning.

4. Do you think Bill's comment about the second company's problems with one of its brands should be considered by the members? Why? Why not? Would you suggest that the members seriously consider the lowest bid? Why? Why not?

5. If a company misses the date for submitting bids, do you think a purchasing group should consider the company's bid when it arrives? Why? Why not?

6. Let's say that Charlie's bid ends up being the same as the first manufacturer. Of the four, which manufacturer do you think the members should choose? Why? Why not?

NOTE

1. Much of the material in the introduction preceding the case information has been adapted from Russell S. Winer, "Organizational Buying Behavior," chapter 5 of *Marketing Management*, 2nd ed. (Upper Saddle River, N.J.: Prentice Hall, 2004).

Distribution Decisions and the Lawson Furniture Company

MANUFACTURERS OF goods have to develop distribution systems that get their products to their respective buyers effectively and efficiently. Channels generally imply physical distribution, or what is called *logistics*. Manufacturers may use direct channels—that is, channels that they control or operate, such as a bank having retail branches and allowing customers to bank online. Or they may use indirect channels—those not controlled or operated by them. These channels must be encouraged by marketing managers to carry the manufacturer's products, just as ultimate customers must be persuaded to buy them. Getting channels to carry and sell a manufacturer's products is a basic activity of channel management and is called *push* strategy. Motivating customers to ask for a manufacturer's products by name is called *pull* strategy.

There are a number of types of marketing intermediaries, including agents, brokers, wholesalers, and retailers, among others. And there are factors that affect a channel system, including the buying behavior of the ultimate consumer, the manufacturer's competitors, the manufacturer's marketing strategy, and the manufacturer's financial resources.

If manufacturers sell directly to the ultimate consumer, this is considered a zero-level channel. A one-level channel includes one intermediary, such as a retailer. A two-level channel contains two intermediaries, such as a wholesaler and a retailer. A three-level channel contains three intermediaries, such as a wholesaler, a jobber, and a retailer.

Marketing managers must help decide on the number of intermediaries to use at each channel level. There are three strategies available: exclusive distribution, selective distribution, and intensive distribution. Exclusive distribution means that the number of intermediaries is limited. It is used when the manufacturer wants greater control over the selling of its products. Selective distribution means that the number of intermediaries is more than a few but less than all who are willing to carry the manufacturer's products. Intensive distribution means that the manufacturer places its products in as many intermediaries as possible.

Manufacturers need to select intermediaries carefully. For instance, they need to learn how many years the company has been in business, the products the company carries, how much the company has grown, what its financial situation is, and where it is located, among other information. This information should be known about a prospective intermediary before it is selected.[1]

THE CASE

The Lawson Furniture Company outside Winston-Salem, North Carolina, manufactures wooden chairs and tables for kitchens. Although these chairs and tables are not expensive compared to some other brands, over the years the company has insisted on maintaining a selective distribution system in the sense that the company chooses furniture store chains and independently owned furniture stores on an individual basis. In essence, the company receives orders from these buyers and then ships the orders directly to the chains and stores. The company has a solid business relationship with the company that ships the furniture, McMann Shipping.

Now, Derrick Lawson, the son of the founder of the company, has become president as a result of his father retiring, and he wants more stores to carry the company's furniture. He realizes that the company can manufacture more units per day. He also realizes, as a result of talking to McMann Shipping, that no matter how many units have to be shipped, McMann can ship them without any problems. McMann guarantees it.

Derrick listened intently as Louise Rogers, the company's marketing director, informed him about a new chain of furniture stores that had opened in several cities in the Southeast.

"This new chain, Furniture Mart, is growing fast. In fact, according to the company's president, Aaron Sims, the officers expect to open 50 new stores in as many cities in the next two years alone."

"Interesting. Right now we are selling to two or three chains and 250 individual stores. According to the plant manager, we can produce enough units to supply another chain or two and at least 250 individual stores. Do you think we should sell to this chain?" Derrick asked.

"I think we should investigate the possibility."

"All right. Make sure you check out where the company wants to locate stores. I don't want to sell our brand to a chain that will have stores close to stores that we already sell to. The managers of those stores wouldn't like it, and rightly so. In addition, find out how the store's salespeople help their customers. Too many furniture stores hire people who have very little knowledge about selling anything, let alone furniture. I've been in several stores recently where the salespeople were just sitting around, not paying any attention to customers. I don't want to sell our brand to stores that have salespeople who do this."

"Okay. I'll have my assistant investigate the company's sales staff by going to one or more stores," Louise told him.

"That's an excellent idea. Ask her to go to at least three stores. She may take a week to do it, but I think what she learns will help us make a decision."

"What if another chain with stores in the same markets as Furniture Mart learns about our interest in selling to Furniture Mart? What if they ask a few questions?"

"We'll worry about that when the time comes. Besides, if Furniture Mart's stores are not that close to the other chain's stores, we'll use that as our excuse."

Two Weeks Later

Derrick entered Louise's office and asked, "Louise, what did you find out?"

"Well, Furniture Mart is interested in opening stores in some markets that have stores that carry our lines. However, based on information that I was provided, the company's stores will not be that close to the competition. Therefore, I think we should offer the company one or more of our lines."

"Do you have the list of cities where they intend to open stores?"

"Yes." Louise glanced at her desk, then picked up a piece of paper and handed it to Derrick.

He looked at the list of cities and nodded. He noticed that Louise had written names of stores that carried one or more lines of Lawson furniture beside some of the cities. "This is excellent work. According to what you've written, Furniture Mart's stores will not have a lot of competitors that carry our brands. In fact, I see no more than five."

"That's correct. Yet, we had discussed trying to sell to stores in most of the cities on the list."

Derrick nodded. "I remember, but I put it on hold because of my father announcing his retirement."

"This may be our best opportunity to get our lines into these markets," Louise said.

"That's a good point. Oh, what about the company's sales staff? Did you have your assistant check several stores?"

"Yes, Maria visited four stores and noticed that most of the salespeople were very professional. As soon as she entered three of the four stores, someone greeted her and asked if she needed help."

"That's good to hear. I tell you what, come up with some figures for me—you know, about how many units the company would be interested in, when we would have to deliver the units, etc., etc. Okay?"

One Week Later

Louise sat down in Derrick's office. "I have the Furniture Mart figures," she said. "The company would be interested in stocking three tables and 12 chairs at each store, for a total of 75 tables and 300 chairs. When the 50 additional stores open, that would increase to 225 tables and 900 chairs."

Derrick nodded. "Very good. I assume they specified a particular table and chair?"

"They said they would be interested in stocking the table and chair that sells the most."

"That would be the smaller table that has room for four people. Did they ask if we would cut the price because of volume?"

"No. I assume they will pay our price."

"Hmmm, I wonder if they will come back—that is, when we get ready to make a deal—and ask for a discount because of volume."

Louise remained silent.

"Well, what do you think?" Derrick asked.

"I think we should make a deal."

"Okay. Let me know what you find out."

One Week Later

Louise was back in Derrick's office. "I informed Furniture Mart that we were interested in selling our best-selling table and chair to them."

"What did they say?"

"They agreed to order the number I mentioned—75 tables and 300 chairs. They did not ask for a price reduction. They also mentioned that whenever a new store opened, they would buy additional tables and chairs."

"Great. When will we receive their first order?"

"Within the next two weeks."

"Good. I'll make sure that we produce enough to fill their order." Derrick smiled and added, "Great work, Louise."

One Month Later

Louise was seated in Derrick's office. "Several independent furniture stores and one chain have found out about Furniture Mart's order and consequently have decided not to order any more furniture from us."

Derrick's jaw tightened. "What happened?"

"Several owners claim that Furniture Mart's stores offer consumers lower prices—prices that they won't or can't match, by the way—and they don't like the idea of selling the same tables and chairs as Furniture Mart's stores. So they cancelled their orders."

"How many stores are we talking about?"

"Five independents, and the chain has 50 stores."

"The independents don't worry me, but the chain does. Fifty stores—that's a lot. Which chain is it?"

"Robertson's."

"Have you contacted Robertson, the owner?"

"No, I thought I should speak to you first."

"Well, contact him as soon as you can; try to persuade him to carry our lines. His company has carried our products for years and years; I don't want to lose his business."

"Okay. I'll let you know what he says."

Louise tried contacting Robertson after she returned to her office, but his secretary informed her that he was out of town and would not return until Friday.

Three Days Later

When Louise called Robertson's office again, the secretary put her call through.

"Mr. Robertson, this is Louise Rogers, the marketing director for the Lawson Furniture Company. We've learned that you intend to stop ordering from us. Is that correct?"

"Yes, Ms. Rogers, that's correct. We understand that you have made a deal with Furniture Mart, which has several stores that compete with ours in several markets. We don't wish to compete directly with Furniture Mart. After all, we have a name that is well known and respected by consumers. In fact, in our last survey, we learned that our customers shopped at our stores because of our name and reputation, not our prices. Our customers know they are getting excellent brands at fair prices. Furniture Mart, on the other hand, has to start out with low prices primarily to establish itself in each market. I predict that they will increase prices once their name is known. However, I do not wish to play their game."

"So you will not place any more orders with us?"

"Ms. Rogers, if you sell to Furniture Mart, your brands may go down in value—at least, among consumers. I don't sell brands that are considered cheap or inferior. And I don't wish to take the risk of this occurring. Understand?"

"Yes, Mr. Robertson, I understand. Does this mean that you will never buy from us again?"

"Probably. Like I said, I don't wish to carry lines of furniture that consumers consider cheap or inferior, and that is what will happen when Furniture Mart starts offering your brand."

"You don't know that for certain, Mr. Robertson."

"Yes, I do, Ms. Rogers. In order to stay in business, I have to know what my competition does." Mr. Robertson sighed then added, "You may wish to check the number of brands that have stopped selling to Furniture Mart."

"What do you mean?"

"I mean that several companies have stopped selling to Furniture Mart."

"Is there anything we can do to persuade you to keep selling our products?"

"If you stop selling to Furniture Mart, we may be interested in carrying your products again."

"Thank you, Mr. Robertson."

Louise Rogers stared at the telephone after she finished her call. Had companies stopped selling to Furniture Mart because of their products' less expensive image created by Furniture Mart's low prices? Or was there another reason? She needed to learn which companies had stopped selling to Furniture Mart and why before she talked to Derrick. If Robertson was correct, Lawson Furniture might change its mind about selling to Furniture Mart.

Louise made several calls and learned that at least three companies had stopped selling to Furniture Mart. One company had stopped because Furniture Mart was several quarters late in its payment. Another company had stopped because of Furniture Mart's low prices; the company feared what the low prices would do to its overall image. Louise was not able to learn the reason for the third company's action.

QUESTIONS

1. Louise Rogers learned that one company had stopped selling its products to Furniture Mart because of the low prices. Based on that information, should she persuade Derrick Lawson to forget about selling to Furniture Mart? Why? Why not?

2. Louise learned that one company had stopped selling its products to Furniture Mart because of late payment. Based on that information, should she persuade Derrick to forget about selling to Furniture Mart? Why? Why not?

3. Since Robertson's says it does not intend to order any more from Lawson Furniture, do you think Lawson Furniture should reconsider selling to Furniture Mart? Why? Why not?

4. Because several independent furniture stores and one chain intend to stop ordering from Lawson Furniture because the company sells to Furniture Mart, do you think the company should continue to sell to Furniture Mart? Why? Why not?

5. Do you think Lawson Furniture may lose additional independent furniture stores? Why? Why not?

6. Do you think Lawson Furniture may lose additional chains of furniture stores? Why? Why not?

7. Do you think selling to Furniture Mart is worth losing a few independent furniture stores and one or more chains of furniture stores? Why? Why not?

8. If you were Louise Rogers, what would you suggest that Lawson Furniture do? Why?

9. Do you think the Robertson chain should try to compete with Furniture Mart's prices? Or do you think Robertson is being hardheaded in his thinking? Why? Why not?

10. Do you think Louise should try to persuade Robertson to carry Lawson's brands in his stores? Why? Why not?

11. What other system could Lawson Furniture use to distribute its products? Is this system better than the one Lawson uses? Why? Why not?

NOTE

1. The introductory information has been adapted from Russell S. Winer, "Channels of Distribution," chapter 10 in *Marketing Management*, 2nd ed. (Upper Saddle River, N.J.: Pearson Prentice Hall, 2004), and Philip Kotler, "Designing and Managing Value Networks and Marketing Channels," chapter 17 in *Marketing Management*, 11th ed. (Upper Saddle River, N.J.: Pearson Prentice Hall, 2003).

AA Motorcycles
Using Sales Promotions

SCOTT PORTER works in the AA Motorcycles marketing department in Cleveland, Ohio. He had learned the history of the company just in case a question or two was asked by Robert Jenkins during the interview for the job a few years back. Now Scott was looking at a photograph of an older AA model, and he remembered that Alexander Atchison had founded the company in 1945, after he had returned from World War II. Scott also remembered that the company hired its first full-time employee the same year. Of course, more employees were hired as the company grew. And the company had either held or entered motorcycle races to test its products and, of course, to get the brand name before the public. In fact, the company had established a racing division early in its history. The company had won numerous races over the years. The racing division had been discontinued, though, when sales decreased in the 1970s.

In 1950 William ("Billy") Atchison, Alexander's younger brother, had joined the company, and the company was incorporated. The same year the company began recruiting more dealers, especially in the Midwest and South. By 1955 the company had several hundred dealers scattered throughout those regions. During that year the company had slightly increased the diameter of the tubular frame so that larger engines could be mounted.

In 1960 the company introduced a sportier bike that was lighter. When consumers learned about it, they went to dealers and test-drove it. Primarily because of its size and comfort, the model's sales exceeded all expectations.

In 1965 the company introduced a model that was similar to the sportier bike but was for off-road operation. At the end of one year, sales figures were greater than anyone had expected.

In the late 1960s and early 1970s, as a result of more Japanese brands of motorcycles entering the United States, sales of AA Motorcycles decreased. Even though the company introduced sportier models and off-road models, none of these had much appeal to motorcycle buyers. In the mid-1970s the company faced a financial dilemma and was sold to a much larger and financially secure company that had investments all over the world. With capital, AA Motorcycles conducted a national survey to determine what motorcycle riders preferred in bikes. Based on the results of the survey, the company designed a sportier bike to compete with the Japanese brands.

The sporty AA Flyer, unveiled in 1979, set the standard for sporty motorcycles. Sleek in appearance, the AA Flyer was unlike its Japanese competitors; it not only looked good, but the seat was larger than those found on competing bikes and consequently was more comfortable. Indeed, riders praised the bike's looks and comfort.

Throughout the 1980s the company introduced more models that focused on looks and comfort. In the 1990s the company expanded its physical facilities in Cleveland and, of course, introduced more models that focused on appearance and comfort.

In 1995 the company celebrated its 50th anniversary. Almost 200,000 riders came to Cleveland, where the company held a party. Articles about the celebration appeared in newspapers and motorcycle magazines. Several stories made the national television networks. As a result of the publicity, sales figures for various models increased.

In the early 2000s, sales figures continued to increase. Indeed, some journalists who wrote for motorcycle magazines claimed that sales were better than expected. However, the average age of those who preferred AA models was the late 40s. Some who wrote for the business press claimed that as the average age of the company's buyers got older, fewer of these folks would be inclined to purchase motorcycles.

THE CASE

Scott Porter had read what the forecasters had written. Now, he put down the photograph of the old AA model and picked up an illustration of a large, plastic, three-wheel toy motorcycle that had been designed for a small child to ride.

Suddenly his boss, Robert Jenkins, entered the office and asked, "What's up, Scott?"

"I'm looking at the illustration of the model that we intend to give away to children if their parents test-drive one of our products," Scott replied.

"You mean the model based on one of our older motorcycles?"

Scott nodded. "Hopefully, when advertised, the model will appeal to young children. And I hope it will cause children to encourage their parents to come in to test-drive the motorcycle that we've designed for adults."

Robert shook his head. "I have my doubts about the idea."

"Why? What's wrong with it?"

"Well, I realize that the model is for children. And I realize that if they see it they will want it. However, will they be able to persuade their parents to drive to an AA dealership to take a test-drive on one of our models? That is the question. On the other hand, let's say that thousands more than we are anticipating go to dealers and request test-drives, just to get models for their children. Dealers would run out, and we would look bad, especially if people started complaining." Robert stopped and scratched his chin. Then he added, "Remember, others in the marketing department had sales promotion ideas, and some of the ideas were very good, maybe better."

"I think this idea may work."

"It may—that is, if the target market learns about it."

"The target market will learn about it; we will have commercials appearing during programs that reach children."

"Okay. But consider the cost of the model. If you remember, each model will cost about $25 to manufacture."

"I know that, but we are limiting the number of models to 45,000; so we are spending under $2 million. Yet, if it causes sales to increase, say, 10,000 or 20,000, it will be worth it."

"Still, I think it's a bad idea."

"Then explain how we are going to attract younger adults. If you look at the demographics of our buyers, well, you know how old they are."

"Yes, I do, and I agree with you; we need to do something that will bring in younger adults, and not just males. Women account for 15 percent of our market now. But I'm not sure this is the best sales promotion idea we can come up with, you know, to reach young adult males and females."

"Then how are we going to attract them?" Scott asked.

"How about a contest or a sweepstakes?" Robert asked.

"We thought about those several months ago. Most of the marketing folks believe this is the best idea at this time. Remember, the target market has to visit the dealer to test-drive a motorcycle. That is the only way parents can get a model for their child."

Robert nodded. "You want to go to lunch? We can discuss it further while we eat."

Scott nodded and followed Robert out of the office. He realized that he had a battle on his hands.

QUESTIONS

1. Out of various sales promotion activities that companies use, do you think the idea mentioned in the case is the best for reaching younger adult males and females? Why? Why not?

2. Do you think Scott will be persuaded by his boss? After all, his boss does not like the idea. Or do you think Scott will stand his ground and insist that the idea be implemented? What would you do if you were in Scott's position?

3. What other sales promotion activities could be used by the company? Which activity would you recommend? How much would it cost to implement? Would it increase sales? If so, by what percentage?

Juan Ortiz Photography

J**UAN ORTIZ,** a 28-year-old Mexican American photographer, opened a small commercial photography studio in June 2004 in a Texas city of 280,000 inhabitants. He purchased photographic equipment and studio furnishings with $12,000 obtained from a loan guaranteed by the Small Business Administration. His personal savings of $6,000 provided working capital that he hoped would be adequate to sustain operations until he began to realize sales revenue. Juan is an above-average photographer with considerable experience in photojournalism in addition to six years experience with a large commercial photography studio that specialized in portrait photography for college and high school yearbooks. His experience with portraiture is his chief reason for establishing a commercial studio, and he plans to specialize in this area by offering quality portraits at affordable prices.

A north–south interstate highway bisects the city and serves as an asphalt barrier between its poorer and more affluent neighborhoods. Ortiz located his studio just east of the highway in the sector inhabited by 97 percent of the city's African American and Hispanic populations. (See table 14.1.) In 2004 the median household income in this sector was $18,000 annually.

Juan realized that establishing any small business in a low-income area would be risky, and even more so in his case, because he is selling a service considered a luxury by most low-income families. He believes the risk is worthwhile because he sees several factors in his favor:

1. He is the first, and only, commercial photographer located east of the interstate, which frees him from immediate competition.
2. Freedom from direct competition allows him to charge lower prices without fear of being undercut by a competitor. He believes this to be a critical factor because he

---

This case was prepared by Joseph R. Pisani, professor emeritus, Department of Advertising, College of Journalism and Communications, University of Florida, Gainesville.

TABLE 14.1
City Populations (and percentages)

	CAUCASIAN	AFRICAN AMERICAN	HISPANIC	OTHER	TOTAL
Western sector	168,640	716	1,456	1,400	172,212
	(80.0%)	(2.3%)	(4.0%)	(70.0%)	(61.5%)
Eastern sector	42,160	30,084	34,944	600	107,788
	(20.0%)	(97.7%)	(96.0%)	(30.0%)	(38.5%)
Totals	210,800	30,000	36,400	2,000	280,000
	(75.3%)	(11.0%)	(13.0%)	(0.7%)	(100.0%)

feels that the current market demand is not sufficient to support more than one photography studio. Cutthroat price competition would result in rapidly declining sales revenues for all competitors, should others enter the market.

3. He is Mexican American, speaks fluent Spanish, and easily empathizes with other Hispanics in the eastern sector, whom he views as his primary market. Because the Caucasian and African American populations in the eastern sector are nearly twice as large as the Hispanic population, he considers them secondary markets that he should not ignore.

4. Hispanic families maintain strong familial ties. They often have large families and are strongly cognizant of the importance of such family occasions as weddings, birthdays, anniversaries, and graduations. He believes that these families would like to record these events as permanent family mementos if photography services are provided at prices they can afford.

5. Hispanic families generally have church weddings, which makes them an excellent market for bridal photography package plans. His experience with bridal photography is limited, but he plans to do a lot more of it, particularly on weekends, to supplement his income from portraiture.

6. The mobility of residents in the eastern sector is limited because many residents do not own motor vehicles. His studio is one block from a city bus stop, and free parking is available in a parking lot directly behind the studio. Nearly 20 percent of his primary market lives within walking distance of the studio. He believes that the mobility problem makes it difficult, if not impossible, for eastern sector residents to patronize western sector commercial photography studios. Also, western sector studios charge 25 to 35 percent higher for work of the same or similar quality.

The first six months of operation, however, were a disappointment. Juan barely broke even. He averaged one wedding every two weeks and only averaged eight portraits per week. His second six months resulted in losses due to a decline in his wedding business. However, his portraiture business doubled during this time. His gross revenue for his first year was $170,000. Expenses totaled $180,000 (expenses included his weekly salary; the amount drawn varied depending on his revenue and expenses for the week). The losses caused him to fall behind on the payments for his SBA loan.

Juan began to realize that his fundamental problem might be that his services were virtually unknown to most residents in the market area. He depended on relatives, friends, and the recommendations of satisfied customers to send him new business. He wants to advertise, but he is in debt already and is considered a poor credit risk by commercial lending institutions.

An SBA official, investigating the reasons for Ortiz's missed loan payments, advised him to apply for a second SBA loan to fund an integrated marketing communications program. The official believed that Ortiz's business plan was sound, but that he lacked the financial resources to advertise his services continuously over at least a six-month period. He explained that sustained advertising would attract a wider customer base. The quality of Ortiz's photography coupled with his reasonable prices would generate the word of mouth referrals needed for repeat business. He suggested that Ortiz write a letter to the SBA requesting the loan, with detailed documentation as to how the money will be spent.

Juan Ortiz's SBA proposal requested a $20,000 loan to cover the costs of creating and producing an integrated marketing communications campaign and placing advertisements in local media continuously for six months. He explained that the increased sales revenues generated by the campaign would allow him to continue the program over the long term. His only advertising expenditure to date was for a listing in the local *Yellow Pages*. This expenditure also entitled him to a complimentary listing in the Yellow Pages Online. Three community newspapers served the eastern sector. The first served the community in general. The second was a Spanish-language paper, and the third reached the African American community. A Spanish-language radio station covered the entire city. Ortiz wanted to place advertisements in these media but couldn't because of his weak financial position.

QUESTIONS

1. Outline an integrated marketing communications plan that you believe Juan Ortiz can use to support his request to the SBA for a $20,000 loan. Include your recommendation for a creative strategy. Be prepared to answer questions asked by your instructor and peers.

2. Propose a media strategy and a media plan that details your recommendations for traditional and nontraditional media that Juan Ortiz can use to spend the $20,000 most efficiently and effectively over a six-month period. Be prepared to answer questions asked by your instructor and peers.

PART III

The Client

Marshall Company's Integrated Marketing Communications Campaign

THE AMERICAN Association of Advertising Agencies (AAAA) views integrated marketing communication (IMC) as "a concept of marketing communications planning that recognizes the added value of a comprehensive plan that evaluates the strategic roles of a variety of communications disciplines—for example, general advertising, direct response, sales promotion and public relations—and combines these disciplines to provide clarity, consistency, and maximum communications' impact through the seamless integration of discrete messages."[1]

Larry Percy defines integrated marketing communications as the planning and execution of all the types of advertising and promotion selected for a brand, service, or company in order to meet a common set of communication objectives, or more particularly, to support a simple "positioning."[2] More recently, William Wells, John Burnett, and Sandra Moriarty have called IMC "the practice of unifying all marketing communication tools, as well as corporate and brand messages, to communicate in a consistent way to and with stakeholder audiences (that is, those who have a stake or interest in the corporation)."[3]

According to Thomas C. O'Guinn, Chris T. Allen, and Richard J. Semenik, integrated marketing communications "is the process of using promotional tools in a unified way so that a synergistic communication effect is created." They add, however, that today "the emphasis on communication is not as important as the emphasis on the brand."[4] Current thinking, then, is about integrated brand promotion (IBP)—that is, using "various communication tools, including advertising, in a coordinated manner to build and maintain brand awareness, identity, and preference."[5] IBP was first discussed by Don E. Schultz and Beth E. Barnes in their book *Strategic Brand Communication Campaigns* (1999).

THE CASE

Clarice Stepps is the vice president of marketing at the Marshall Company, which produces several lines of clothing. D. G. Jeans, its best-selling line, is carried by several national retail giants such as J. C. Penny and Sears.

Clarice looked at her watch. She was late for the meeting with account executive Carolyn Sparks at the advertising agency that handled Marshall's D. G. Jeans account.

"I'm sorry I'm late, but the traffic was crazy," she said.

Carolyn smiled and said, "Clarice, don't worry about it. Please, sit down. You remember Bill Mathis, one of our top creative directors."

Clarice nodded. "Good to see you again, Bill."

"I'd like to introduce Mary Scott, one of our top copywriters, and Steve Lambert, one of our top media directors."

"Good to meet you," Clarice said and shook hands with each of them.

"Bill will present the new campaign for Marshall's brand of jeans," Carolyn said, "and Steve will present the media expenditures. Mary is on hand in case you have questions about the copy."

"I'm certainly looking forward to the presentation," Clarice said. "As you recall, our last campaign for D. G. went nowhere. In fact, sales have decreased 2 percent since last quarter."

Carolyn nodded, but she didn't say anything. Instead, Bill Mathis said, "Why don't we begin?"

Clarice listened attentively as Bill elaborated on the campaign theme: "being carefree and responsible" (both at the same time). He discussed three 30-second television commercials that emphasized both ideas (carefree and responsible). The commercials featured the same woman in various situations, including running after and holding a little girl. The woman was dressed in D. G. Jeans. Bill waited while Clarice read the scripts for the commercials. Then he grabbed four print ads and explained each one. All featured the woman and child from the television commercials and emphasized the theme. Next, he discussed the company's website, which would be used to promote the jeans. In fact, the website would contain the three television commercials in their entirety. Bill explained that people would be directed to the website whenever they visited websites for retailers such as J. C. Penny and Sears. He discussed public relations, which would be used to promote the theme, the brand, and the company. The public relations aspect of the campaign would be done by the ad agency's sister company, which was located in the same building but on a different floor.

Bill then turned to Steve Lambert, who presented the media expenditures, which totaled more than Clarice had budgeted for the campaign.

"Steve, the total for media is more than our total budget," Clarice said.

Steve looked at Bill and Carolyn.

Bill said, "We could cut some of the media or, if you prefer, the public relations aspect of the campaign; however, you will be losing an important tool. Right now, we have a cohesive, synergistic campaign. If you decide to eliminate one of the tools, such as public relations, because of the cost, it could decrease the value of your brand."

Clarice nodded, understanding, but said, "Bill, the total for the media alone is several million dollars over my budget for the campaign. You know that. I'm sure that Carolyn informed you before you started. What am I supposed to do? Go back to my office and ask for more money?"

Bill nodded and said, "Yes. You said earlier that sales have decreased 2 percent since last quarter. Apparently something's wrong. People have forgotten your brand, or they have never heard of it."

"Or they have grown tired of it," Clarice said.

"If that's the case," Bill said, "then you need this campaign more than ever. This campaign puts a new spin on an old brand." Bill waited for her to say something, but she didn't. "Why don't you try to get more funding before you ask me to cut something from the campaign?" he asked.

Clarice didn't care for Bill's question, so she didn't reply, but she thought he was probably correct in his assessment of the campaign. Each tool was being used well to deliver the theme and the brand, and the media that Steve had selected would reach the intended target market. If they cut some of the media, the message might not be received. Nonetheless, she had misgivings about going to her boss and asking for several million dollars. Her budget had been increased substantially in one year alone. In fact, based on what her boss said, her budget was the largest it had ever been in the history of the company.

Bill said, "Remember, Clarice, this campaign has been developed for the fall and holiday season. We will need to know something within a few days."

QUESTIONS

1. Do you think a company like Marshall needs a cohesive, synergistic, integrated campaign in order to sell jeans? Why? Why not? What are companies that produce jeans doing as far as advertising is concerned? Be prepared to explain at least one company's advertising effort.

2. Do you think Bill should have suggested that Clarice ask for additional funding?

3. Do you think Bill should have developed a less expensive campaign—a campaign that was based on Clarice's budget?

4. Do you think Carolyn, the account executive, should have said something when Clarice indicated that Bill should have known what the budget was? If so, what should she have said?

5. Do you think Clarice will ask for more funding when she returns to her office? Why? Why not?

6. Do you think Clarice will request that one or more communications tools be cut from the campaign because of funding?

7. Do you think Clarice will request that some of the media be cut, knowing that the message may not be received by a sizable audience?

8. Put yourself in Clarice's position at the end of the case. What would you do? Why? Explain.

9. Let's say that Clarice gets the additional funding for the campaign. Do you think one campaign can be so successful that it increases sales more than 2 percent in one quarter? Be prepared to support your answer by providing an actual case. (Remember, this campaign is for fall and the holiday season only—that is, one quarter.)

NOTES

1. Philip Kotler, *A Framework for Marketing Management* (Upper Saddle River, N.J.: Prentice Hall, 2001), 280.

2. Larry Percy, *Strategies for Implementing Integrated Marketing Communications* (Lincolnwood, Ill: NTC Business Books, 1997), 2.

3. William Wells, John Burnett, and Sandra Moriarty, *Advertising Principles and Practice*, 6th ed. (Upper Saddle River, N.J.: Prentice Hall, 2003), 536.

4. Thomas C. O'Guinn, Chris T. Allen, and Richard J. Semenik, *Advertising and Integrated Brand Promotion*, 3rd ed. (Mason, Ohio: South-Western, 2003), 37.

5. Guinn, Allen, and Semenik, *Advertising and Integrated Brand Promotion*.

Objectives, Strategies, Tactics, and the Bogie II

BEFORE ADVERTISING agency personnel place ads and commercials in the media, they have to develop advertising *objectives*. These will guide the integrated marketing communications plan, including the development of the ads and commercials.

Advertising objectives serve several purposes. They help with decision making, especially in the selection of creative strategies, tactics, media, and the budget. They also help by providing specifics against which the campaign can be measured. Indeed, advertising objectives should be measurable or quantifiable. They should include measures that can be used to evaluate the effectiveness of the campaign.

Sound advertising objectives will express what the various aspects of the campaign are to accomplish. The objectives will communicate specific tasks. For instance, an advertiser's objective may be to increase consumer awareness about a product or brand, or to change consumers' beliefs or attitudes about a product or brand, or to increase a product's or brand's sales, or to stimulate trial use of a product or brand. Of course, there are other objectives an advertiser may try to achieve.

According to Russell Colley, "a goal is an objective that has been made specific as to time and degree." He writes, "An advertising goal is a specific communication task, to be accomplished among a defined audience to a given degree in a given period of time."[1]

Once an advertising objective has been written, advertising personnel can develop a creative *strategy* that will help them create print advertisements, commercials, and other kinds of advertising or promotion. Basically, a creative strategy determines what the advertising message should communicate to the intended target market.

A creative strategy must consider the advertiser, the advertiser's advertising or promotion problem, the target market, the product or service, the major selling idea or benefit, and the campaign theme, among other topics.

After the creative strategy has been developed, advertising personnel must think about what *tactics* to use. Tactics are actions or executions that bring the strategic idea to life. Basically, a tactic or execution is the way an advertising appeal is presented in advertisements, commercials, and other kinds of advertising or promotion, and there are numerous ways advertising messages can be presented. Humor, dramatization, animation, testimonial, slice of life, demonstration, and straight sell are some of the more popular tactics or executions that have been employed over the years.

THE BOGIE

In 1965, in England, Alec Bogart designed a small car called the Bogie. A year later he unveiled the prototype. The car was fuel efficient and easily carried four people. The Bogie went into production in 1966, and when it was introduced to the public, the public did not know what to make of it. To some, it looked like an MG; to others, it looked like a Mini Cooper. However, consumers eventually purchased it. After all, it was a safe, comfortable, small car that could be driven easily around town. In 1970 the car was brought to the United States, where the press was skeptical about it.

The Old Bogie

The Bogie was modified and customized by companies in the United States. Indeed, it was driven in races, eventually winning several. As a result of the publicity, many consumers, especially celebrities, purchased Bogies. However, the Bogie was pulled from the market in the United States in 1972 because of sales. Some claim that the real reason it was pulled was that it failed to meet emissions regulations.

Nonetheless, it continued to sell in the United Kingdom. Three million had been manufactured by 1973. Although sales were not as high as for other brands, special editions of Bogies were introduced occasionally. These special editions caused enough consumers to purchase the car to keep it in production. Eventually the car had a cult following. Four million Bogies had been manufactured by 1980 and 5 million by 1985.

The New Bogie

After 1985 the company that manufactured the Bogie had financial problems. By 1990 these financial problems had worsened considerably. The company was purchased by a larger conglomerate that manufactured various brands of cars and trucks. In 1992 the conglomerate changed the name of the small car to the Bogie II.

In 1995 the conglomerate introduced a new fuel-injection and bigger engine. The car, which was still small but three inches longer and two inches wider, featured airbags for the driver and passenger and side impact bars in both doors. In 1998 a newer version was unveiled at an auto show in London. In 2000 a new Bogie II was unveiled at an auto show in Detroit. Later the same year the sporty small car was unveiled at an auto show in Paris.

In 2005 the newest Bogie II was brought to dealers in the United States, selling about 25,000 within a year and a half, which was better than executives' expectations, considering that the brand had not been in front of the American public for several decades. In order to maintain sales, the company introduced new models, including the Bogie II Convertible in 2006. The company announced that other models would appear in the United States later.

THE CASE

John Martin was the marketing director for the Bogie II USA Division and was responsible for overseeing the marketing of the car in the United States. Now he was examining an earlier campaign and remembered that the advertising agency's challenge had been to help make the brand become an icon in the United States, much like it was in the United Kingdom.

The agency showcased the car's shape as well as its name in an innovative campaign that stood out. The campaign consisted of outdoor and print advertising in 50 of the largest markets in the United States. These markets corresponded to dealer locations. Ten of the 50 markets were given special consideration, primarily because of the number of dealers and the profile of the populations in these markets.

Outdoor bulletins were greatly used, along with urban wall murals and several different forms of street furniture, including panels placed on newsracks, public telephone stands, and public benches. Bus shelters were used, too, especially in the 10 key markets. Urban wall murals were used within Chicago, Los Angeles, and New York City. Street kiosks were used in San Francisco and Seattle. Airport kiosks and objects such as garbage cans, newspaper vending machines, and pay phones emphasized "Although small in size, it's big where it counts." The creative was changed every week in certain markets. One humorous television commercial appeared, once during the Super Bowl.

John remembered that the old campaign achieved an average reach of 90 percent within the 10 key markets and an average 80 percent reach in the other markets. The campaign was successful; dealers had consumers waiting for weeks for their cars.

He thought that the first campaign for the Bogie II Convertible—"Nothing like it in the whole wide world"—continued in the humorous vein. He wondered how the agency would advertise the newest Bogie II Convertible. If the agency targeted women, men might not want to be associated with it. If the agency targeted men, women might not care for it. Yet men accounted for more than 65 percent of the Bogie IIs sold in the United States. Of course, some of these men probably bought the cars for their wives or daughters.

The team from the agency would be arriving soon to present their proposed campaign. John was anxious to see what they had created.

QUESTIONS

1. If you worked for the agency that handled the Bogie II Convertible, what advertising objectives would you develop for advertising the newest model? Explain the rationale for your objectives.
2. If you worked for the agency that handled the Bogie II Convertible, what creative strategy would you develop for advertising the newest model? What is the creative strategy's purpose? Explain the rationale for your creative strategy.
3. If you worked for the agency that handled the Bogie II Convertible, what creative tactics (executions) would you use for advertising the newest model? Explain.
4. Can you think of another advertising objective? If so, what is it?
5. Can you think of another creative strategy? If so, what is it? What is its purpose? Explain the rationale for this creative strategy.
6. Can you think of another tactic? If so, what is it? What is its purpose? Explain.
7. Do you think the agency should continue in the humorous vein? Why? Why not?
8. If you think the agency should change its focus—that is, do something other than humor—explain the focus and provide the rationale for it.

NOTE

1. Russell H. Colley, *Defining Advertising Goals for Measured Advertising Results* (New York: Association of National Advertisers, 1961), 6.

Bank of Ayden
Advertising Management in a Small Market

THE TOWN OF Ayden, Virginia, is like many small towns in rural America. Once a thriving railroad terminus, the town had lived through the Depression, World War II, and various cycles of economic boom and bust. Whereas Ayden had been a self-contained town of approximately 8,000 people 50 years ago, it was now a "bedroom community" to a large city, Richmond, that had grown toward it. Within the Richmond city limits lived about 500,000 people, and another 500,000 lived in the surrounding counties. Ayden, just 35 miles from downtown Richmond, had become a popular place for those working in downtown Richmond to live. This was because the school system was well regarded, serious crime seemed less likely to occur, property taxes were low, and a wide range of housing options were available to persons of every income level.

Ayden, like many small towns in Virginia, had an old "downtown" of small shops, older restaurants, and some light industry. The car dealers had all moved to adjacent locations on State Highway 48, as had many of the other businesses and retailers and fast-food restaurants found in the typical small town. Highway 48 was also the location of the main office of the Bank of Ayden. (They didn't refer to their offices as "branches.") The bank had three other offices, one in the older downtown, one a drive-thru near the interstate, and another full-service office in nearby Harcourt Hills, the most expensive housing development in Ayden. This office, located on the western side of Ayden, was the fastest growing office within the Bank of Ayden system.

The Bank of Ayden had been formed in the early 1950s by a group of prominent local people. At the time, the First National Bank of Ayden was the only bank in town. The early years saw some nasty local infighting among the ownership groups of the two banks as each sought to keep up with the capital and banking needs of the citizens of Ayden.

In 1972 the Bank of Ayden was the first bank in Ayden to have a drive-thru window. In 1975 it was first again with ATM machines at every office. As 1980 began, the Bank of Ayden made a strategic decision to "automate"—their term for the sizable investment they made in computers and electronic banking capability. In the mid-1990s, the bank beat its marketplace rivals with a website, Internet banking, and automatic bill-paying services.

While First National Bank of Ayden was always seen as the primary competitor, several other start-up banks were chartered during the Bank of Ayden's first 30 years. These included Harcourt Bank, First Federal Bank and Trust, Bright Star Financial, and Martin County Bank. (Ayden is located in Martin County, Virginia.) All of these banks were doing relatively well, but the momentum fueled by innovation and aggressiveness was clearly on the side of the Bank of Ayden. As the bank celebrated its 50th anniversary, executives had every reason to be cautiously optimistic about the future of Ayden and the bank.

As Richmond spread toward Ayden, many large multilocation bank holding companies took notice of Ayden and its growing population. In the 1950s, most people who lived in small towns also worked in those towns. This made the selection of a local bank an easy choice. Paychecks were deposited and cashed monthly, savings accounts were set up, and the limited array of bank services that were then allowed by regulators were readily obtained from banks where the employees probably knew your name. Often, the president of these banks was a highly visible community leader. It was not uncommon for this same individual to be a member of the local country club, a member of the hospital board of directors and the school board, and a member of several community organizations, such as Kiwanis Club and Rotary International.

As banking laws changed, banks were able to offer mortgage loans, credit cards, investment services, direct deposit services, investment banking services, and more. Many small-town people now worked outside the city limits in which they lived, and the appearance of such national and regional bank chains as Bank of America, Wachovia, and Bank One contributed to making banking a commodity service.

Within the city limits of Ayden there were now branches of five banking chains: SouthTrust, SunTrust, Bank of America, Wachovia, and Wells Fargo. Each had at least two offices. Each of these bigger banks had the advantage of more local marketing dollars to spend, national advertising campaigns running in the major markets (like Richmond), and the appearance of more sophistication, more technology, and better-trained staffs.

Actually, the Bank of Ayden had better-trained personnel, better office locations, the same broad range of financial services, and par or superior electronic capability. It also enjoyed lower staff turnover, lower or no fees on everyday services, and better-than-market rates on CDs and deposit accounts. In other words, on paper, the other local banks and the mega-banks didn't effectively compare with Bank of Ayden.

But this was on paper. Bank of Ayden president Covington Smith clearly saw the challenge. Each of the chain banks had branches in Richmond, and Bank of Ayden didn't. Given the growing population of people who mostly did not grow up in Ayden, he worried about the future. All of the people who were moving to Ayden already had banking relationships with *someone*, often with one of the mega-banks in another city. Moving to Ayden simply meant a different branch office; the move didn't necessitate new accounts, a new bank, or a new relationship. Covey knew that he did not have the marketing and advertising dollars to compete with the larger banks. He also knew that he had a bank that on most measures could compete with, and in most cases better, the products and services of the chains.

One day, at an Ayden Hospital board of directors meeting, Covey asked another board member, "Who created your new logo and corporate identity package?"

"Trumpet Pickle Creative, in Richmond," was the answer. "Give them a call. They've done great work for my company."

The next day Covey called Trumpet Pickle Creative. About three days later, he met with the agency's managing partner. Two days later, Covey received an e-mail from Trumpet Pickle outlining a general approach for positioning the Bank of Ayden within its marketplace, and from that positioning, for creating messaging to give the bank more visibility through an ongoing marketing, advertising, and communications program. (See box 17.1.)

As Covey reviewed the Trumpet Pickle document, he made a list of the available media possibilities in Ayden. These would all be local media, with television coverage coming from Richmond, since Ayden was in the Richmond DMA.

His list showed:

- The *Ayden Gazette*, a weekly town newspaper.
- Two low-power local AM radio stations.
- Outdoor advertising.

The next day Covey called Trumpet Pickle to tell the agency that he needed a couple of days to think through the outline. He then formed the fundamental questions he had been wrestling with: "How can the Bank of Ayden mount a marketing, advertising, and communications program with so few media options available in Ayden? How could Bank of Ayden compete with the better-known larger banks? How could Bank of Ayden become the primary bank for newcomers to Ayden?"

QUESTIONS

1. What is a DMA?
2. Is it realistic to think that Bank of Ayden can compete with the larger banks?

BOX 17.1

Bank of Ayden Marketing Outline and Budget

The following outline of tasks and activities is presented in rough chronological order, with an approximate budget shown. Actual estimates will be provided as work begins.

Establish a Marketing Committee

Form a 5–6 member committee that includes Covey Smith and Pickle Trumpet Creative as permanent members. Other committee members serve a 12-month term. The committee meets formally on a quarterly basis for no more than 1 hour.

The purposes of the committee are to (1) demonstrate to the employees the importance of marketing and that it is everyone's job, (2) provide a resource for market intelligence, and (3) provide a sounding board for marketing and advertising activity.

Estimate: $2,400 (to cover the managing partner's time for four quarterly meetings each year).

Emphasis Period Calendar and Internal Communications Program

This is developed in cooperation with the Marketing Committee. The purpose of the calendar is to focus internal attention on certain products, services, and marketing programs. This calendar also drives in-office signage and support materials as needed. Likewise, it provides a reference point for advertising and planning. Once the calendar is completed, Trumpet Pickle Creative will be better able to estimate marketing and advertising costs for all the elements of an emphasis period.

Media Audit

Trumpet Pickle Creative will perform a Media Audit to identify traditional and nontraditional media options for advertising placement. This will include, but not be limited to, newspaper, cable television, radio, outdoor, and sponsorships.

Estimate: $2,000 one-time expense.

Create a Positioning Statement

A positioning statement identifies the place that the Bank of Ayden (BOA) wants to occupy in people's minds. Its purpose is to identify a unique niche that is supportable by the substance and actions of BOA. When completed, this Positioning Statement will differentiate BOA from competitors, and it will form the basis for a Positioning Line.

Estimate: $1,200–1,500.

Positioning Line

Over the years, BOA has used positioning lines such as "The Best in Community Banking," "We're Your Neighbor," "Bankers and Neighbors," and "Building Tomorrow Together."

A new Positioning Line needs to come from a new Positioning Statement. The new Positioning Line will define BOA to all of its important constituencies. This line will also suggest a copy platform for all internal and external communications.

Estimate: $1,200–1,500.

Advertising Creative Brief

This document will be prepared by Trumpet Pickle Creative and approved by BOA. It will establish the framework for the development of a copy platform and a creative "look and feel" for BOA messaging. By establishing what needs to be done creatively, the Creative Brief becomes an ongoing reference point for all ads, outdoor advertising, direct mail, website work, collateral materials, and in-office point-of-purchase materials.

Estimate: $500.

Bank of Ayden Audiences

- Customers
- Prospects
- Employees
- Professionals (lawyers, CPAs)
- Shareholders
- Martin County

Creative Development

BOA has identified the following creative needs:

- Trust Department ad
- Rate ad for deposits
- Free online banking ad
- Outdoor advertising board design
- Website home page (possibly)
- Bank services folder
- Direct mail campaign

Estimate: $17,000–23,000 (excludes printing).

This budget covers only the items mentioned above by BOA. As the Marketing Calendar is developed, Trumpet Pickle and the Marketing Committee will likely recommend other elements so that a complete marketing program for each Emphasis Period can be built.

Cross-Sell Opportunities

Using the BOA database and other resources, Trumpet Pickle will evaluate and price programs for cross-selling BOA products and services. These will be tied in to established Emphasis Periods. Among the programs and initiatives we will look at are:

- Office point-of-sale signage system
- E-mail marketing program
- Electronic and hard-copy newsletters

Estimate: TBD. Detailed estimates will be provided for programs BOA wants Trumpet Pickle to investigate.

3. How do banks compete? What do customers really want from a bank?
4. Is there anything missing from the Trumpet Pickle outline?
5. Covey thinks "The Oldest Bank in Ayden" is a strong positioning for the bank. What do you think?
6. Who is the target audience for Bank of Ayden?
7. Covey wants the bank to remain independent. Do you think this is realistic or possible? Should he consider selling the bank to one of the larger competitors or to another large bank looking to move into Ayden?

F. T. Beverages and Marketing Strategy

MARKETING STRATEGY concerns the customer, the corporation, and of course the corporation's competition. Companies use marketing strategies in order to differentiate themselves from their competitors in the minds of consumers.

According to Subhash Jain, in order to create a marketing strategy, a company must make three decisions:

1. *Where to compete*; that is, it requires a definition of the market (for example, competing across an entire market or in one or more segments).
2. *How to compete*; that is, it requires a means for competing (for example, introducing a new product to meet a customer need or establishing a new position for an existing product).
3. *When to compete*; that is, it requires timing of market entry (for example, being first in the market or waiting until primary demand is established).[1]

Numerous companies have used various models of marketing strategy over the years. Michael E. Porter, in his book *Competitive Strategy: Techniques for Analyzing Industries and Competitors*, identifies three generic marketing strategies: overall cost leadership, differentiation, and focus.[2]

Overall cost leadership is based on price reductions and promotional deals. Companies cannot compete by lowering prices alone, however, because the competition may match or even beat their prices.

Differentiation is based on positioning such unique or valued marketing mix dimensions as product, price, distribution, or marketing communications. As M. Joseph Sirgy writes, "the manner in which a marketing manager emphasizes or de-emphasizes certain elements of the marketing mix is . . . positioning."[3] Sirgy lists various positioning techniques according to the most emphasized element of the marketing mix:

Positioning strategies emphasizing the *product*:

- Positioning by product class
- Positioning by product attribute
- Positioning by intangible factor
- Positioning by competitors
- Positioning by country of origin

Positioning strategies emphasizing *price*:

- Positioning by relative price

Positioning strategies emphasizing *distribution*:

- Positioning by brand-distributor tie-ins
- Positioning by distributor location
- Positioning by distributor service

Positioning strategies emphasizing *marketing communication*:

- Positioning by celebrity or spokesperson
- Positioning by lifestyle or personality[4]

Companies may use any of the above techniques to position their brand (products or services). Of course, the techniques selected must be relevant to the company and its products or services.

Focus, Porter's third generic marketing strategy, is based on concentration—that is, appealing to a particular buyer group or a narrowly defined target market. According to Sirgy, three positioning strategies apply to focus:

- Positioning by customer benefit or problem
- Positioning by user or customer image
- Positioning by use or application[5]

THE CASE

Lois McRoberts, vice president of marketing at F. T. Beverages, has been working for the company for almost five years and has seen two ad agencies service her account, which is the company's leading product, a fruit-and-tea-flavored drink that competes against other fruit-flavored products. Although the product caused a stir when it was introduced almost 15 years ago, its sales decreased about 5 percent last year, which caused the company's senior management to shake their heads and wonder what happened to the brand. The company also considered looking for another ad agency.

As Lois explained to her bosses, research studies have found that young consumers, especially those 13 to 17 years old, tend to be fickle because of their desire to experiment. They like to explore other flavors and drinks. Consequently, they are not as loyal to a particular brand as older consumers. After briefing senior management, Lois was assigned the task of asking the company's ad agency to launch a more modern ad campaign, one that would appeal to young consumers, especially the 13-to-17-year-old group. Now she was examining several ideas that the agency had proposed.

The first idea was a positioning strategy that emphasized the product's physical attributes. Three different television commercials that targeted 13-to-17-year-olds would consist of dizzying colors that represented the various fruit and tea flavors; the dizzying colors would come to life, and each would represent a specific ethnic group. Each commercial would have a young announcer's voice describe the ingredients and state why the drinks were different from those of the competition.

The second idea was a positioning strategy that emphasized marketing communication by a celebrity spokesperson. Three different television commercials would feature a young popular female singer who had a hit television program on one of the cable networks. The program was one of the most watched by the 13-to-17-year-old target market. Each commercial would be a slice of life that resembled the singer's television program. However, each commercial would end with the singer reaching for one of the company's fruit-and-tea-flavored drinks.

The third idea was a positioning strategy that emphasized customer benefits. Three different television commercials would feature the fruit-and-tea-flavored drinks' primary ingredients. Each commercial would focus on a different benefit. For instance, one commercial would focus on the product "being cool," while another would focus on the product "being a healthier alternative to regular soft drinks." Another would focus on the product "being refreshing."

As Lois studied the ideas, she wondered if any of the ideas would appeal to the 13-to-17-year-old target market and consequently increase sales. She examined the first idea again. Although she liked the idea about the colors representing the various fruit and tea flavors and then coming to life and representing specific ethnic groups, she wondered if describing the product's ingredients and providing a reason for the product being different was enough to persuade the 13-to-17-year-old age group to buy the product.

Lois examined the second idea again. She had seen the young singer's popular television program several times. As a result of its popularity, the singer had signed contracts with various advertisers. This was a problem, at least to Lois. If the singer starred in the commercials and the commercials were seen by the 13-to-17-year-old age group, how many viewers would associate the singer with the brand? To Lois, this was crucial. If viewers did not associate the singer with the brand, a lot of money would have been wasted on hiring the singer.

Lois examined the third idea again. Although it was similar to the first in the sense that the product's ingredients would be featured, Lois realized that the benefits mentioned had been used by other advertisers, including her competition. She thought that other benefits could be emphasized.

Lois wondered if she should accept one of the ideas or inform the account executive at the agency that she wanted more ideas.

QUESTIONS

As you consider the following questions, remember what Lois said about young people not being loyal to a specific brand.

1. What do you think Lois will do? Why?
2. What would you do if you were in her shoes? Why?
3. Do you think the agency came up with some good ideas based on positioning? Explain the basis for your judgment.
4. Formulate another idea based on positioning that you think would be more appealing to the 13-to-17-year-old target market. Why is your idea better?
5. Do you think positioning is the best strategy for a fruit-and-tea-flavored drink? Why? Why not? Think of another strategy concept and explain it.
6. Find an article about a similar product that describes the current marketing strategy or plan. (Check *Advertising Age*, *AdWeek*, or *BrandWeek* magazines first. They contain articles about various companies and their products.) Then explain why you think the marketing strategy or plan worked, or why it didn't.

NOTES

1. Subhash C. Jain, *Marketing Planning and Strategy*, 6th ed. (Cincinnati, Ohio: South-Western College Publishing, 2000), 23.

2. Michael E. Porter, *Competitive Strategy: Techniques for Analyzing Industries and Competitors* (New York: Free Press, 1980).

3. M. Joseph Sirgy, *Integrated Marketing Communications: A Systems Approach* (Upper Saddle River, N.J.: Prentice Hall, 1998), 74.

4. Sirgy, *Integrated Marketing Communications*, 74.

5. Sirgy, *Integrated Marketing Communications*, 96.

Payroll Sure Acquires 2XPayday
Naming the New Company

DAVID HILL, chief marketing officer of BigIdeaz, a growing advertising agency in a large northeastern city, has just heard the news on the business segment of the local public radio station: 2XPayday, the fifth largest such company in the country, was bought by Payroll Sure, the third largest company in the category. Combined, the new company could challenge the number-two company, DirectPay, whose size is three times that of the new company.

Both companies, and their respective managements, were firm believers in advertising and promotion. Each company had grown quickly over the past few years, led aggressively by their respective CEOs. Now that they had merged, it was almost certain that the new company would continue to aggressively seek growth as it sought to catch up to DirectPay.

Dave was almost certain that part of the reason for the merger was an intention to "go public" in the future. Both 2XPayday and Payroll Sure were privately owned. Dave made a mental note to learn all he could about each company, and the new company. There is nothing he would like better than to have his agency, BigIdeaz, invited to pitch for the new company's marketing and advertising account.

2XPAYDAY

Patty Marshall, a CPA by training, founded 2XPayday eight years ago, and it quickly grew through aggressive marketing, sound products, and the smart leadership that Patty provided. From the outset, Patty decided to target companies with fewer than 50 employees, offering their management a turnkey payroll processing solution. Through a highly motivated and well-compensated sales force, 2XPayday grew by double-digit percentages every year. At the time that 2XPayday was acquired by Payroll Sure, it had almost 75 employees, more than 4,000 accounts, and a reputation for personal attention and fair pricing.

One of the most time-intensive tasks any small business has to contend with is payroll processing. Generally, employees of most small companies are paid every two weeks or twice each month. Getting checks to employees might seem simple, but an employer has to withhold federal and state taxes, any contribution the employee makes to a health care program, social security taxes, perhaps two 401k contributions (one from the employee, one from the employer), and other deductions authorized by the employee. In addition, the employer must pay a payroll tax for each employee that must be calculated based on the employee's compensation level. When all of this is done, if the company offers direct deposit, deposits have to be made to employees' individual accounts at their banks. And this may have to be done twice each month, or even more frequently.

At the end of each year, the employer has to provide W-2 statements to each employee showing his or her compensation for the year, along with all deductions. This is not only time consuming and very important to each employee, but there can be penalties imposed on the company, or lawsuits brought by employees, if the record keeping is sloppy or inaccurate.

For these reasons, many companies choose to outsource their payroll processing. The costs are generally reasonable, and the time saved and potential problems that can be avoided can be significant.

2XPayday's computer system and technology base had grown over the years, and it was considered current and capable. As you might imagine, any company in the payroll processing business *must* have a robust and technically capable computer system if it is to compete effectively. 2XPayday had such a system, and the addition of a dedicated sales force that added a "personal touch" to the sales process made 2XPayday an easy company for customers to deal with. Any issues and challenges that the sales force could not handle could usually be handled by a very professional and qualified group of customer service representatives. In sales materials produced by the company, 2XPayday described itself as having a "high-tech *and* high-touch" approach to payroll processing.

2XPayday's CEO, Patty Marshall, was an entrepreneur to the core. While in college she had started a campus computer dating business that had quickly become profitable and successful. To do such a thing on a conservative college campus, amid hecklers and a suspicious college administration, was the result of a very strong personality and drive for success. Whenever Patty had to defend her on-campus business against those who saw it as "demeaning," "un-cool," and "unnecessary," she held her ground and took on the most strident challengers. This was not a woman to be told she couldn't do something. This is the way she built and ran 2XPayday. Her personal drive and creativity was responsible for many of 2XPayday's software innovations, products, and customer service programs.

PAYROLL SURE

Payroll Sure was founded two years earlier than 2XPayday by Jim Sinclair, an electrical engineer by training. During the early years, Payroll Sure approached business the same way 2XPayday did—"high-tech and high-touch." In fact, many in the industry would tell you that Patty used the early success of Payroll Sure as the model around which she built 2XPayday.

Five years after being founded, Payroll Sure acquired a small payroll processing company in the Midwest. Two years after that, it acquired another payroll start-up company in the South. These acquisitions allowed Payroll Sure to grow faster than 2XPayday, and in the process it allowed Payroll Sure to gain a technological edge on almost everyone in the payroll processing category. An early adopter of new technology, Jim Sinclair also acquired another small payroll processing company that was on the leading edge of using the Internet. He bought it solely for the technology and the company's experience that had allowed it to do business entirely over the Internet.

This acquisition fascinated Jim, and he reengineered his company to be an Internet-only payroll provider. This meant that customers had no choice but to "call-in" payroll using a computer and the Internet. Most of the other companies allowed customers to make a choice as to how they sent payroll data for processing; they could use the telephone, a fax machine, or the Internet.

Most competitors thought that the Internet-only switch was a risky move by Payroll Sure, but the growth of the company after taking this step was the envy of the category. Taking such a risk made Jim Sinclair an industry "darling," and he was a much sought-after speaker at technology conventions and technology fairs. This visibility, added to his somewhat flamboyant personality, and significant financial success, reinforced his self-opinion that he knew almost everything there was to know about payroll processing in today's computer age. "Acquire and grow, acquire and grow" was his mantra, and the effectiveness with which Jim applied it spoke for itself.

THE ACQUISITION OF 2XPAYDAY BY PAYROLL SURE

Jim Sinclair had known Patty Marshall for several years through industry meetings and by reputation. Twice in the past, Jim had approached Patty about acquiring 2XPayday. Each time, Patty politely told him it was not for sale.

Three months ago Jim asked again, and this time Patty decided to sell 2XPayday to Payroll Sure. The transaction was a complicated one, but Patty got $8 million over five years and a minority ownership stake in Payroll Sure, and she had to sign an agreement to stay with the new company as the chief technology officer. Part of her new responsibilities involved merging the two companies' technology bases, eliminating redundant products, and building a sales infrastructure to grow the company.

Publicly, and in the trade magazines, Jim Sinclair made it clear that "all existing ideas" were open for review as the new company took shape, that Patty was an equal voice in shaping the new company, and that "the best practices of each company" would be retained. He even went so far as to say that the name of the new company was up for grabs, and that there were precedents for all the naming options. Should the new name be either Payroll Sure or 2XPayday Payroll Processing, or should an entirely new name be considered?

Patty, thinking about the expanded company, made a list of what she considered the biggest issues:

1. Which company's product names should be used?
2. What size companies should the new company go after?
3. How should the all-Internet selling approach of Payroll Sure be blended with the human-contact sales force approach of 2XPayday?
4. What should the name of the new company be? Why?

So far, Patty and Jim were getting along fine. Both were excited about the new company and its growth possibilities. Both had plenty to do. And both felt that they knew the best way to proceed.

QUESTIONS

1. What does your "gut" tell you about this situation?
2. Why do you think Patty Marshall finally sold 2XPayday?
3. Do you think either company has a better way to sell payroll services?
4. What makes Jim Sinclair tick?
5. How should Patty approach the new company's product mix?
6. Can the two sales cultures be blended? Why, or why not?
7. Do you think the goal of "going public" is realistic?
8. What are the pros and cons of each name? Is there any information that you don't know that you wish you had?
9. Will a new name be the best option?
10. What would you recommend the company's new name be?
11. Any suggestions for Dave Hill at BigIdeaz Advertising?

Montana Cool
A Potential New Product Disaster

MONTANA COOL was the name given to a line of tropical sportswear made from fabric that contained a revolutionary new fiber treatment that improved each garment's breathability in hot weather. The result was a product that withstood wrinkling, always looked crisp and cool, and actually kept the wearer more comfortable. There was nothing else on the market like the Montana Cool line in terms of colors, styles, number of items, and "look." Finally, someone had produced a fresh idea and execution in the highly competitive line of upscale fashion apparel for next year's summer season.

In the apparel business there is a long lead time from the first showing of new items to their appearance in retail stores. Generally, spring and summer fashions are introduced at industry trade shows in late summer or early fall of the previous year. In other words, the Montana Cool line of fashionable "resort wear" would first be seen by retail merchandise buyers about seven months before it started to arrive at retailers. Based on the appeal and interest in a particular line or item as demonstrated by potential buyer reaction at trade shows, the company offering the new items would then contract for manufacturing. Sometimes the offering company would have no manufacturing capability and would simply "source" a manufacturer to meet its specifications. Sometimes the offerer would be an apparel manufacturing company that would then start the process of ordering the fabric, programming for production, and building inventory.

In the case of Montana Cool, the company behind the brand was a major apparel manufacturer that was well known in the industry. Already it produced several noncompeting lines of apparel—coats, suits, and hats for example—that were category leaders in sales and reputation. And while producing a new line of tropical resort wear would be a new direction for the company, there was every expectation that the new line would be a success, based on research conducted with consumers and retailers.

THE LAUNCH OF A NEW BRAND

In the apparel industry, one of the largest trade shows for new spring and summer fashions occurs in early September of the previous year. It was now early June, three months before the trade show, and the manufacturing company that owned the Montana Cool brand was meeting with its advertising agency to tell them what support and materials it needed to launch Montana Cool at the September trade show.

The manufacturer outlined the needs as follows:

- Four-color trade ads run in September trade publications.
- A catalog of the entire line of Montana Cool apparel for distribution at the September trade show.
- Designs and artwork for a trade show booth.
- An update about Montana Cool for the manufacturer's website.
- A sales kit for the manufacturer's sales force to use when making sales calls on customers and prospects.
- A brochure for use by the sales force and distribution at the trade show.
- Giveaway items for the trade show showing the name Montana Cool.

As the ad agency team drove back to its office, they knew that it would be a busy next few months.

MONTANA COOL BUDGET AND WORK SCHEDULE

Two of the first steps that the agency needed to take were to provide "budgets" to the client for each project and a timetable for completion. A budget is an approximate, educated guess at the cost of a project. It is generally made by an ad agency based on its experience with similar projects in the past. It is usually expressed in round numbers and contains few details. This is only natural and reasonable since the agency does not have an approved concept to price, or know how many ads are needed, or how many pages there will be in the catalog or brochure. This is a dangerous place for an ad agency, because the client can sometimes take budgets for actual "estimates." Estimates, when done correctly, are detailed breakdowns of line-item by line-item costs that make up an entire job. Estimates should show such details as photography costs (if any), printing costs (when the number of pages and the production quantity run is known), artwork and mechanical costs (when it is known how large each project is), and outside costs such as travel, research, models, and other items.

The Montana Cool group had indicated that they had a total figure budgeted for all the work that the agency was being asked to produce. They declined to provide it, however; rather, they asked the agency to tell them how much all of the listed work would cost.

When an agency is at this point, it must decide how to provide the numbers that the client wants. Should the agency estimate low in order to ensure that it gets the work? Should the agency estimate high, to establish a "value" for its work, then adjust downward if the estimate is over the client's budget total? An agency would not want to give a quick-answer total only to find that the client was prepared to spend more. The more the client is able to spend, the more flexibility the agency has to recommend creative executions that might cost more but produce better results. This is a fine line to walk.

After much discussion, the team members decided to provide the following figures for what they thought would be needed to concept each project. The agency's account manager, Ralph Ames, would stress to the client that the figures did not reflect any outside costs such as printing, travel, and so forth, and that they were *an educated guess* based on historical information at the agency.

Four-color trade ad campaign	$60,000 (incl. photography)
Product catalog	$15,000 (concept/time only)
Trade show booth	$12,000 (concept/time only)
Website update	$3,500 (concept/time only)
Sales kit	$6,500 (concept/time only)
Brochure	$5,500 (concept/time only)
Giveaway items at trade show	$2,500 (concept/time only)
TOTAL	$105,000

The agency then worked on the timetable. The first project to schedule was the trade ads. Closing dates for most trade publications are about 30 days prior to the month of publication, so the agency had to have the ads completed, approved, and sent to all trade magazines by early August. This meant that there were only seven, or at most eight, weeks available to get the ads produced.

The product catalog would take about two weeks to print, as would the brochure. This meant that there were about 10–12 weeks available to design and create mechanical artwork for these two projects. The trade show design and artwork would have to be completed in time to produce the actual trade show booth. The trade show vendor had told the agency that the manufacturing of these panels had to be started no later than 60 days prior to the trade show setup date (generally one week before the show begins).

There was plenty of time for the website update, which had to be completed and online by the start of the trade show, and for the giveaway items that generally took about four weeks to produce.

The manufacturer's sales force would begin sales calls about three weeks before the trade show, sometime in mid-August. This gave the agency about 60 days to design and produce sales kits for the sales force.

While there was not a great deal of extra time, the schedule for creation and production of all materials to support the trade show launch of Montana Cool could be met if everyone understood the dates involved.

THE AD AGENCY BEGINS WORK

Since the timeframe to create and produce the trade ads was the most critical, that is where the agency started. It was decided to recommend a three-ad campaign: one ad focused on the decision to introduce Montana Cool, one focused on the technology of Montana Cool, and one focused on the sportswear line itself. Copy and layouts were prepared in about two weeks by the agency's creative department for presentation to the client. The "look" of the entire campaign and product introduction would be driven by these ads, so early approval by the client was important. As was the agency's policy, a formal detailed estimate was provided for the client's ad manager for all jobs at the same time.

It took another week for the client's ad manager to show the layouts to senior management for final approval. At the same time he gave the agency approval to proceed with the ads, he also returned all of the other job estimates approved and signed.

Immediately, the agency began to make plans for the necessary photography. This took longer than it should have because the photographer that the agency wanted to use was on vacation until after July 4. This meant that if the photography could be taken right after the photographer returned from vacation, allowing time for selection of the images and color correction of the shots, and for the creation of mechanical art, there would be very little margin for error if the ads needed to get to the trade magazines by early August. Of course, once the ads were ready for sending, there would be a final round of client approvals needed.

On July 10, the photography was shot on location in another city. By Friday, July 19, the agency had the color corrected images for the three ads. These were shown to the client, who requested further color work on one of the images. On July 23, the client approved all photography so the ads could be assembled. The first closing date for one of the trade magazines was August 1. This is the date by which the magazine needed to have the ad in hand so that it could appear in the September issue. The agency called for an extension, if possible. The magazine moved the closing date to August 6. On Friday, July 26, the art director working on the trade ads left for a week's vacation. Earlier, the agency creative director had asked the art director to change her plans. She said she couldn't, because she was going on a cruise that had already been paid for.

Fortunately, in the week prior to leaving for vacation, the art director assigned to the project had gotten another art director involved. This was not an ideal situation, to change art directors at the 11th hour, but the agency had little choice if it was to meet the upcoming August 6 deadline. Things were getting a little tense at the agency, but most people had seen this happen before.

MONDAY MORNING, JULY 29

At about 10 a.m., Account Manager Ralph Ames got a call from the ad manager asking him to attend an emergency meeting at the client's offices. When he asked about the purpose for the meeting, the ad manager cut him off with a curt, "You'll see."

"Great," thought Ralph, "what a way to start the week."

Before leaving, Ralph thought it might be a good idea to "pull time"—that is, check with the agency's accounting system to see how much time and other costs were in the trade ads job to date. A quick look revealed that, to date, photography and retouching costs totaled $28,000, travel and other expenses for the photo shoot totaled $2,500, and copy, layout, and mechanical art totaled about $36,000. Doing a quick mental review, Ralph knew that the three ads had to be sized for six different magazines, and that only one set of sizings had taken place to meet the one magazine's closing deadline now set for August 6. Putting the printouts in his briefcase, Ralph left for the client's office.

What he walked into was a very tense meeting room where no one spoke until the ad manager started the meeting by announcing, "We have just been advised by our legal department that the name Montana Cool has been previously registered and we cannot use it. We'll have to come up with a new name."

With more than a hint of sarcasm, the ad manager added: "Anyone have any suggestions?"

QUESTIONS

1. How could this have happened? Whose responsibility do you think it should be to clear a product name for use?
2. Go to the website www.uspto.com. What is the USPTO, and what does it do?
3. Should Ralph be worried about the estimate for the trade ads? Should he bring up the status of that job?
4. If you were in Ralph's shoes, what questions would you ask?
5. What options does the ad agency have?
6. What options does the manufacturing company have?
7. It is too late to cancel the September ads due in just a few days. What should be done?
8. Are there any restrictions or considerations that should be raised before a new name is chosen?
9. What is the worst thing you think can happen going forward?

Mickey's, Incorporated
The Client and Its Ad Agency

MICKEY'S VICE president of marketing looked out the window at the snow on the ground and reflected on the company's founder, Mickey Metzman, a man he admired. Mickey was born in New York City in 1930. Although his mother died when he was 10, his father, Marvin, tried to keep the family together. With no education to speak of, Marvin was constantly in search of work; consequently, the family moved often from one city to another. Marvin also remarried more than once, which put a strain on his relationship with Mickey. Mickey spent the summers with his maternal grandmother in New Jersey. His grandmother was a huge influence on him.

When Mickey was in his teens he worked in a restaurant in Indianapolis, Indiana; he enjoyed his job. Three years later he found work in a restaurant in Muncie, Indiana. His father decided to move the family again, but Mickey decided to remain in Muncie. He moved into a boardinghouse and quit school to work full time. (He regretted quitting school, however; in fact, this decision bothered him so greatly that he earned his GED years later while living in retirement in South Carolina.)

Mickey served in the U.S. Army during the Korean War, managing an officer's club. When he was released, he returned to Muncie, where he learned that his former boss had purchased several restaurants in Cincinnati, Ohio. In 1965 the owner of the restaurant offered Mickey the opportunity to try to save the failing restaurants in Cincinnati. Mickey accepted the offer and succeeded. The owner sold the restaurants for a small fortune and shared the profit with Mickey.

Mickey opened the first Mickey's restaurant in Cincinnati in 1970. Mickey's was unique among sit-down hamburger restaurants: the hamburgers were prepared from fresh ground beef and sirloin steak. A year later he opened a second Mickey's restaurant in Cincinnati. This restaurant introduced a curb service: customers could order from their cars, and the orders would be brought to them. In addition to offering various hamburgers, Mickey's offered chili, various "platters," and dinner entrees. Over the next few years, the business grew, and each restaurant featured carpeted dining rooms and comfortable booths.

In 1980 Mickey's offered stock to the public for the first time. In 1982 the company expanded across the border when its 250th restaurant opened in Toronto, Ontario. Three years later, with 500 restaurants, the company celebrated its 15th anniversary. The company introduced a salad bar as part of its celebration. In 1988 Mickey relinquished the day-to-day operations of the company. A year later Mickey's saw its 1,000th restaurant open. In 1990, as a result of an award-winning advertising campaign, the company enjoyed one of its most successful years ever. The company had been in business for 20 years and had more than 1,500 restaurants in the United States and abroad.

However, in 1992, after several mistakes and sagging sales, the newly appointed president of the company urged Mickey to return to the company. Mickey visited managers all over the country and listened intently as they discussed problems. As a result, the company developed a new kitchen that allowed employees to prepare food faster, and it deleted slow-selling items from the menu. After a customer survey was done, newer items were added. In 1995 Mickey started appearing in commercials for the company. He became so popular as a result of his friendly face and relaxed delivery that he appeared in commercials for nearly 10 years. The number of restaurants grew. In 2000 the number of restaurants totaled 2,500. Although Mickey died in 2005, the company did not fail in its mission to listen to customers and introduce new items to the menu.

The vice president of marketing looked at a photograph of Mickey that the founder had autographed for him several years before. He thought about Mickey again. In addition to starring in more than 500 commercials for the company, Mickey had donated his time and money to worthy causes. He supported various charitable organizations and numerous hospitals. He supported numerous foundations and schools, including universities.

The VP picked up a sales chart for the last quarter: sales at Mickey's had dipped about two percentage points. He thought about the advertising agency that handled the company's account. Trident had been the agency for the past 15 years. Although it had created some outstanding work for the company over the years, the agency was about to move its in-house media-buying service to a company that the VP did not like. But Trident, like many other advertising agencies today, was part of a conglomerate, and many executives who work for a conglomerate try to eliminate the duplication of functions across the conglomerate's companies. Their executives ask, "Do we need to offer the same services in all our agencies?" The answer is, "Of course not."

Mickey's vice president of marketing knew a number of employees at Trident and liked them. They were honest, and they worked hard. Even though he had expressed his opposition about the move to several key executives, he had not been able to persuade them to change their plan. Now, he was faced with a major decision: should he suggest that Mickey's stay with Trident or look for another advertising agency? Would Trident's executives actually risk losing a $100 million a year account?

QUESTIONS

This case concerns several issues, including friendship between key executives (advertising agency and advertiser), loyalty between the key executives at the agency and the advertiser, communication between the key executives at the agency and the advertiser, the business practices of conglomerates, and the decisions marketing personnel may not wish to make.

1. Should the vice president of marketing consider the effect of the founder, Mickey Metzman, on the company and its culture with regard to its advertising? How long and to what extent should the company's marketing efforts be guided by the founder's footsteps?
2. Should an advertiser's marketing executives allow their personal relationships with ad agency executives to interfere with or influence their professional decisions?
3. Is the practice of downsizing by conglomerates logical? Ethical? Professional? Can this practice be costly to the company overall? How? Why? Why not?
4. What should the vice president of marketing for Mickey's do? Should he suggest that Mickey's stay with Trident? Should he suggest that Mickey's find another ad agency? Should he be concerned about his friends at Trident possibly losing their jobs as a result of losing a major account?
5. How long can an advertising agency stay fresh on an account? Is there a limit? Support your responses with actual examples.

Venus Motor Sales
Time to Change the Advertising?

ACCORDING TO the company's website, Venus Motor Sales was created with one idea in mind: to build a car for women. Many pundits for automobile publications criticized the idea, claiming that building cars for women was not smart marketing. The idea for Venus Motor Sales germinated in 1995; however, primarily because of careful planning, the company was not founded until 1997. The first car with the Venus name was not built until three years later. The first cars were the V Series. The V2, a sporty truck, was built in 2001. In 2002 the company produced its 500,000th car, a two-door coupe. The same year, Venus unveiled its new V3 Series sedans, coupes, and trucks.

Over the years, Venus earned numerous awards and recognitions, including the following:

2001—the Venus coupe is named "Best Car" in the $10,000–$15,000 category by an independent organization.

2002—Venus is identified as the highest-ranking domestic nameplate, according to an independent organization.

2003—several consumer magazines identify the Venus sedan among the "Best Buys in Compact Class."

2004—Venus ranks number one among all nameplates in an independent organization's evaluation of sales and satisfaction.

2005—Venus ranks number one in sales and satisfaction for the second consecutive year.

And the awards and recognitions continue. Of course, the company's overall success is the result of its well-built economical cars and its competitive pricing strategy, which is clearly evident on each sticker. When you purchase a Venus, you do not have to argue over price.

THE CASE

Now, the company is producing the V4 Series (sedan, coupe, and truck), which has replaced the company's V3 Series and which has been advertised to young people, especially young women. In fact, the company's advertising agency, which was awarded the $200 million advertising account in 2003, created several commercials that targeted young people. These advertisements were based on such high school and college activities as senior trips, dances, athletic events, and sorority functions, among others. The ads appeared in magazines targeting young women; commercials appeared on several television programs that targeted young women.

The vice president of marketing for Venus Motor Sales realized that the company had made a major decision by approving what the advertising agency had recommended and created, but questions were bothering her. As she examined the sales figures for the V4 Series (sedan, coupe, and truck), she knew something wasn't working. This year, sales of the V4 models were down more than 40 percent compared to sales of the V3 Series two years before. Were the advertisements targeting the wrong market? Or, if the market was correct, were the advertisements reaching it? And were the advertisements' messages the right messages? The VP wondered if these messages were breaking through the advertising clutter. She also wondered if the advertising agency had conducted any pre-tests for the ads. Should the agency be instructed to conduct a few post-tests for the advertising?

She looked at the sales figures again and thought, *Of course, the V4 brand is relatively new; it may take longer for it to catch on with consumers.* But the questions continued. Was the brand being advertised appropriately and to the right market? Was it being advertised on the right networks and the right programs?

QUESTIONS

1. Would pre-tests have been the key to whether the advertising message in the current advertisements is the right message? Explain.
2. Is the V4 Series being advertised to the right group of consumers? Why, or why not?
3. Is the media selection—magazines and television—the best selection possible to reach the intended target market? What other options do you think the agency considered?

4. Should the advertising agency conduct post-tests for the advertising, to determine whether it is doing what the agency people think it is doing? Why, or why not? What alternatives are there to post-testing?
5. What else could the advertising agency do to increase brand recognition or awareness?
6. Does it make sense for the vice president of marketing to consider changing agencies? What are the pros and cons of changing agencies at this point?

CASE 23

Neptune Aquatic Club
Marketing and Advertising the Nonprofit Organization

CONGRATULATIONS, Mr. President. Now, what are you going to do?" These were the words that greeted Al Jenson as he walked into the kitchen of his home. An hour earlier, Al had been elected president of Neptune Aquatic Club (NAC), the swim club where his daughter swam competitively.

"I knew the board of directors was going to elect you president last week. I hope you'll be able to devote the time it'll take to help the club grow." With that, Al's wife, Nan, laughed and added, "You've always been a sucker for a good time."

"Thanks," said Al, "I must be out of my mind."

NEPTUNE AQUATIC CLUB

Founded in the mid 1970s, NAC was a year-round competitive swim team. The team, part of U.S. Swimming, trained in a state-of-the-art facility in a mid-sized town in Virginia. With 210 swimmers, ranging in age from 8 to 18, NAC was a very strong team. Often ranked among the elite amateur programs in the United States, the club often saw its graduates go to college on swimming scholarships. Numerous times club swimmers had been invited to the U.S. Olympic Swimming Trials to try for the powerful U.S. Olympic Swim Team.

Running the team was Head Coach Jim Minor, a former college swimmer who had been an assistant at NAC for several years. Several times, Coach Minor had been selected as U.S. Swimming's Southeastern Coach of the Year. One full-time assistant and two part-time volunteer coaches assisted him.

Fees at the club ranged from $60 a month for the youngest swimmers to more than $150 for the oldest. On top of this, the club usually traveled to a swim meet every other month. That meant hotel, travel, and food expenses on top of the monthly fee. So, despite not needing much equipment, year-round competitive swimming can be an expensive sport.

A program of the caliber of NAC's requires a healthy cash flow to meet overhead expenses and coaching salaries. First, there was rental of the pool where the team trained. This facility was owned by the city of Neptune. Then there was insurance, telephone, annual club dues to U.S. Swimming and the sport's sanctioning body, and the other monthly expenses required to operate the club.

There were two important keys to a financially successful club. One was to have more than 250 swimmers, and the other was to have an effective fund-raising program. Having 250 swimmers seemed easy in a town like Neptune, where more than 400,000 people lived in the metropolitan area. But this was not the case. Year-round swimming, especially for younger swimmers, requires a sizable time commitment from parents willing to transport their swimmers to and from practice. The popularity of Little League Baseball, lacrosse, and especially soccer, none of which required the expense or daily involvement of busy parents, made the recruitment of young swimmers somewhat difficult.

Fund raising was a necessary part of keeping the club financially solvent. Generally, this took place whenever NAC hosted a swim meet in Neptune. By getting local businesses or individuals to sponsor parts of or the entire meet, the club could give these sponsors visibility in exchange for cash, services, or merchandise. If a sponsor donated snacks or soft drinks, for example, NAC could then sell these as refreshments to those attending the swim meet.

On weekends when there were swim meets at NAC, the club published a "heat sheet" that told the swimmers from all the teams participating which heat of which event they would swim in. Generally, but depending on the size of the swim meet, there were five or six heats for every event in every age group. The size of the heat sheet allowed the club to sell advertising space within it to Neptune businesses. Typically, the restaurants and motels that were close to the pool purchased these ads.

AL JENSON

Al Jenson, the newly elected president of NAC, was also a successful marketing executive in Neptune. Neither Al nor any other of the club's officers or directors was compensated for serving as part of the club's leadership. Even though they were not paid, they worked hard to provide Coach Minor with the recruits, tools, and financial stability to keep the club successful. Al estimated that during the next year, he would spend in excess of 500 hours working for NAC. This was in addition to the 50 hours per week Al spent at his job as director of marketing for Picnic Foodstuffs, a company headquartered in Neptune that sold and distributed "casual" food products such as chili, hotdogs, and snack foods.

AL JENSON'S CHALLENGE

Very simply, Al had been elected president of NAC to (1) increase the number of swimmers from the current level of about 210 to 260 and (2) put in place a fund-raising program that could be run by the parents to raise money for NAC. The board of directors reasoned that since Al was in marketing, worked for a company that sold the kinds of food they could resell at swim meets to raise money, and seemed to possess high energy and personal interest in the club, he would be a good president. You know, "successful at one thing, successful at all."

At Picnic Foodstuffs, Al had a multimillion dollar budget to support his efforts. At NAC, there was no budget or money available. At Picnic, Al had 20 salespeople and two administrative assistants. At NAC, all salespeople (generally the one or two willing to make sales calls) were parents who volunteered to try selling sponsorships or ads, and there was no administrative help.

As Al thought about what had to be done, he felt confident that he could motivate the club's parents for fund raising, ad sales, and swimmer recruiting. His only question was, "How?"

QUESTIONS

1. Do you think the same advertising and marketing principles apply for selling Picnic Foodstuffs products and a swim club? Why, or why not?
2. What might be different about managing a marketing department and managing a volunteer organization?
3. How would you manage NAC's resources to recruit swimmers?
4. How would traditional advertising tools work to recruit swimmers? Families?
5. What nontraditional tools could be used to recruit swimmers? Families?
6. Why would Neptune's businesses support NAC? Which ones should Al target first?
7. How is not-for-profit advertising and marketing the same as for-profit advertising and marketing? How is it different?

Perkins Advertising
Will Ethics Be a Problem?

BOB SMITH, a recent graduate from a well-respected university, considered himself very fortunate. In spite of a tough economy, Bob had landed a job as an assistant account executive with Perkins Advertising and had almost completed the company's mandatory three-week training program for all new entry-level hires. After tomorrow's classes, Bob will take a test, and upon successful completion he will be assigned to an account group where he will begin the advertising career he studied about in college.

Perkins Advertising is an aggressive, fast-paced marketing communications company founded 27 years ago. With published billings of $40 million, Perkins is one of the largest agencies in the region. The agency is "full-service," meaning it provides its clients with a wide range of marketing, public relations, and creative services. The agency's staff of 35 people has an eclectic mixture of experience, accomplishment, and capability that makes it the "agency of choice" for area college graduates.

An assistant account executive generally provides administrative and account service backup to an account executive. With experience and demonstrated performance, an assistant account executive may be promoted to account executive, then to account manager, and then to account supervisor, managing several account managers. The importance of a good account executive and account manager cannot be overstated: he or she is the primary contact with the agency's client company. As such, he or she is expected to provide account leadership, guiding the client and the client's company to success in the marketplace.

Imagine the account team as the hub of a wheel that has as its spokes the following areas from within the agency to support the client's business: research, account planning, public relations, media, accounting, and creative. It is the account team's job to manage agency services and deliverables to help the client meet specific marketing and advertising challenges.

The account team's relationship with the client sets the stage for what Perkins hopes will be an *enduring and **profitable*** relationship for the agency. This is the key point that Perkins management has stressed repeatedly over the past three weeks. Perkins Advertising is in business to earn *a fair and reasonable profit*. With only one exception during the early years, the agency has been able to operate profitably. This has allowed it to attract and retain qualified people, grow and expand without borrowing, and provide a working environment that is the envy of other ad agencies in the region.

As is the case at many ad agencies, a performance and reward system is in place to assess each account group's performance. Based on the growth of billings (sales) to a client and the profitability of the relationship, or lack thereof, the careers of account team members will rise or fall. Everyone knows this, just as each account group knows the individual account performance standards they are measured on.

Kelly Perkins, founder of the agency, had recently assumed the title of chairman of the board as she relinquished day-to-day management activities to her daughter Katie. As the new president and CEO of Perkins Advertising, Katie was anxious to impart her "stamp" on the agency that her mother founded.

Like many professional people in their late 40s, Katie had attended college in the mid-1970s. Highly principled and distrustful of authority, Katie managed to graduate despite her reputation as a mediocre student and campus troublemaker. After several years as a teacher, an airline flight attendant, and then a yoga instructor, she became an honors graduate from a very competitive, nationally recognized business school. Katie had a "no holds barred" approach to business and the management of people. Tough, demanding, and competitive, she focused on results, even if, at times, some of her peers thought questionable means may have been used.

Katie was also known as someone who was anxious to take the credit but always pass the blame to someone else. Virtually everyone who worked at Perkins Advertising was aware of the very different styles and operating philosophies of the two women. The staff was split 50/50 on whether Katie's style would be better for the agency than had been Kelly's, which had successfully guided the agency for 27 years. In fact, Kelly Perkins had told the trainees that her office was "always open" and that everyone was always welcome to come to her with any business-related ideas or concerns. The senior Perkins seemed approachable, and to Bob's knowledge, her business integrity had never been questioned at any time during the 27 years she had managed the agency.

As the end of Bob's formal training neared, Bob was hoping that he would be assigned to work in Todd Phillips's account group and had been doing some low-key lobbying to get placed there. The agency's largest and most glamorous account, Woltz Industries, was in Todd's group, and many new junior account people viewed it as a fast track to promotion. This perception was further reinforced by the fact that Katie Perkins had been the senior executive on the Woltz account for many years before her latest promotion to president and CEO.

As Bob gained information on the different account groups at Perkins (there were four), he was struck by a confusing set of conflicting data. Both directly and indirectly, Bob had heard that Katie, while managing the Woltz account, had turned her back on a number of "irregular" billing practices regarding what Woltz Industries was billed for agency services. This included the arbitrary inflation of estimates for services given to Woltz before jobs were begun, the falsifying of time-sheet entries that detailed who spent how much time working on Woltz jobs, and the padding of travel expenses for which Perkins was reimbursed. No one seemed particularly troubled by what was going on, explaining that the pressure to make and keep accounts profitable and growing made this something that "all agencies do." Besides, if Katie Perkins, now the agency's president, had allowed these actions to continue while she was managing the Woltz account, it must be okay.

Bob had worked very hard to get his job at Perkins, and he had been working even harder to distinguish himself in the three-week training session. In fact, there was already a "buzz" that Bob was Perkins's next superstar in the making. But as Bob studied for his final examination, a number of troubling questions were rattling around in his head, and he felt that he couldn't ignore them for long.

QUESTIONS

1. Should Bob continue his lobbying efforts to be assigned to Todd's account group?
2. Should Bob ask Todd if what he has heard about the Woltz account is true?
3. Should Bob ask to talk to Katie to fully understand agency billing practices?
4. Several other junior account executives advised Bob not to rock the boat. Should Bob go along with what seems to be accepted agency practice?
5. Should Bob take advantage of Kelly Perkins's standing "open office" invitation and ask her about agency practice?
6. What is ethical behavior?
7. How do ad agencies usually get compensated for their work?
8. What are standard billing practices at advertising agencies?
9. What is an assistant account executive expected to do?
10. Is ambition a bad quality?
11. What are the risks (and rewards) of "going over someone's head"?
12. Whose responsibility is ethical behavior? Are there varying standards and measurement methods?

Professional Advertising and Marilyn Bright, M.D.

FOR MANY YEARS, professional associations such as the American Medical Association (AMA) and the American Bar Association (ABA) limited advertising by their members. Indeed, both organizations claimed that advertising and promotion lowered the status of their professions. However, the codes of these organizations eventually came under fire by state and federal regulatory agencies as well as by several groups that represented consumers. In 1982 the U.S. Supreme Court upheld a Federal Trade Commission order that allowed dentists and physicians to advertise.

Today, the AMA and ABA have guidelines for members who wish to advertise. These guidelines, if followed, will help members who advertise maintain certain standards of the professions and prevent misleading or deceptive advertisements. For instance, the AMA guidelines regarding advertising include the following:

> There are no restrictions on advertising by physicians except those that can be specifically justified to protect the public from deceptive practices. A physician may publicize him or herself as a physician through any commercial publicity or other form of public communication (including any newspaper, magazine, telephone directory, radio, television, direct mail, or other advertising) provided that the communication shall not be misleading because of the omission of necessary material information, shall not contain any false or misleading statement, or shall not otherwise operate to deceive. . . . The communication may include (1) the educational background of the physician, (2) the basis on which fees are determined (including charges for specific services), (3) available credit or other methods of payment, and (4) any other non-deceptive information.[1]

THE CASE

Marilyn Bright, M.D., moved to Miami, Florida, after several years of practicing in Boston, Massachusetts. Specializing in plastic surgery, she was eager to start practicing in Miami. Besides, she had been given an opportunity that comes along once in a lifetime; she had been offered an office for a reasonable price in a small medical building that had three other physicians whose specialties were in areas other than plastic surgery.

After six months of seeing only a few patients, she was determined to increase her practice. She joined two professional organizations and three social organizations. The latter had hundreds of members and generally had professional speakers at the monthly meetings. For one of the social organizations, Dr. Bright spoke about the sun and what it could do to the skin. She addressed the members about her profession and specifically the services she provided. Soon after her presentation her practice grew, but only for a few months, and most of the new patients were one-timers—they came for a specific procedure and did not return.

Although she had ethical questions about using advertisements to promote her practice, she asked her colleagues if they would be interested in advertising their services through one or more print advertisements. They mentioned that they did not like physicians using advertising to promote their practices and suggested that she seriously consider the image that advertising might create for her and the medical profession.

Dr. Bright thought about the issues. Her colleagues had a point, but her practice was not growing—at least, not as she desired. Besides, through one of the social organizations she belonged to, she had met Russell Smith, a young designer who, after having worked for one of the largest advertising agencies in Florida, owned a small design firm that specialized in creating advertisements for print. She contacted Smith, and he said he would prepare rough layouts for three advertisements that she could consider.

When they met in Smith's office, he handed the first rough to her. "As you can see, we incorporated your ideas into the roughs. For instance, this one has a simple headline at the top. The headline will be something like 'Botox Injections.' The headline will be followed by a block of copy that describes the procedure. A second block of copy will describe other procedures. A brief block of copy will contain your name, degree, and certifications. Your business logo, along with the address and phone number, will be at the bottom. A large photograph of a woman walking on the beach will be on the left. Attractive, she will be facing the copy." Smith looked at Dr. Bright as if he expected her to say something. "What do you think?"

"Well, I like the idea for the headline and the blocks of copy, but I'm not so sure about the photograph. Photographs like that have been used by too many plastic surgeons, especially in South Florida."

"But the photograph presents an image that most women desire. This is the reason we're suggesting it."

Dr. Bright thought about what Smith had said, then said, "Okay." Yet, she had misgivings about it.

Smith showed her the next rough. "In this one, we have a headline that goes across the copy and the artwork, except the artwork is on the right-hand side. Again, the headline will be simple and mention a procedure such as 'Liposuction' or 'Breast Augmentation,' followed by a block of copy that describes the procedure mentioned in the headline. A second block of copy will describe other procedures. A brief block of copy will list your name, degree, and certifications. Your business logo, address, and phone number will be at the bottom."

"Do you have an idea for the artwork?"

"Yes. We will have a photograph of a woman in a bikini, seated on the beach. She will be at an angle, so the reader can see the shape of her breasts and her legs."

"Hmmm, such a shot has possibilities, especially if we use a headline like 'Breast Augmentation.'"

"I agree. Now, let's look at the third rough." Smith put the layout in front of her. "This one features you."

"What do you mean?"

"I mean I think we need to introduce who you are, what your credentials are, and what procedures you specialize in. We will have a headline and a photograph of you that introduces you. The photograph will be to the right of the headline and blocks of copy. A block of copy that presents your credentials will be under the headline. A second block of copy that describes the procedures you perform will immediately follow. Your business logo, address, and phone number will be at the bottom."

"Hmmm. I don't know about this one."

"You don't have to decide now. Why don't you take these with you and look at them in your spare time. Then let me know what you decide. Okay?"

Dr. Bright nodded.

"One more thing, if you decide on one or more of these, I'll be sure they are placed with the appropriate media."

"You would do that for me?"

Smith smiled. "That's part of what we do. Here, let me put these roughs in a folder for you, so they'll be easier to handle."

"Thanks. By the way, what do you think about advertising on television?"

"Well, you may have a lot of waste."

"Waste? What do you mean?"

"I mean that television reaches all educational levels and age groups, depending on which program and which station or network you choose. You may spend money reaching audiences that have no need for your services."

"Hmmm."

"However, why don't you speak to an advertising representative from the local cable company?"

"Why the cable company? Why not an advertising agency?"

"An advertising agency will charge you more money to produce a commercial and place it. The cable company can shoot a commercial for very little money. And your representative can place it on several cable channels, not just one, if you buy a package."

"Package? What's a package?"

"Cable companies offer businesses in their areas the opportunity to advertise on television for very little money, comparatively speaking. So they offer packages—that is, they will allow businesses to have their commercials air on three, four, or five different programs on three, four, or five different cable channels—at a relatively low cost. The cost depends on how many programs on how many channels the commercial airs. And, of course, for how many weeks the commercial airs."

"You mean I can have a commercial air on several cable channels for a certain period?"

"That's right. For instance, depending on the package, your commercial could air on Lifetime, Arts and Entertainment, Hallmark, and other cable channels that appeal to a similar market. Placed properly, your commercial could reach primarily adult females."

"Hmmm, I didn't know that. Thanks, Russell."

"If you decide to speak to the cable company's advertising representative, be sure to ask to see the programs' ratings and the demographics of the viewers. You don't want to advertise to people who are not part of your target market."

Dr. Bright put the folder on the back seat of her car and fastened her seatbelt. She glanced at the clock on the dashboard and realized that she could be home before 5 p.m., depending on the traffic.

QUESTIONS

1. Let's say Dr. Bright considers the roughs again and decides to use at least two. Which ones do you think she should use? Why? Why should she not use the other one?

2. Let's say that after Dr. Bright runs one or more of the print advertisements in the local newspaper and a local magazine, the other physicians in her building criticize her. Then they ask her to stop running the advertisements. What do you think Dr. Bright should say or do? Why?

3. Let's say Dr. Bright informs her colleagues that she needs to advertise in order to grow her practice. However, they inform her that she needs to stop advertising, that they do not advertise and do not wish to, and that if she continues she will have to move out. What do you think Dr. Bright should do? Stop advertising? Move out? Explain.

4. Let's say Dr. Bright contacts the local cable company, and an advertising representative explains that the cable company can produce a commercial and place it on several cable channels' programs, for an incredibly low price. Do you think she should seriously consider this proposition? Why, or why not?

5. Do you think Dr. Bright should contact an advertising agency before she decides to go with the cable company? Why, or why not?

6. Do you think Dr. Bright should use print advertising or cable television advertising, or both? Why? Explain.

NOTE

1. American Medical Association guidelines, "E-5.02 Advertising and Publicity," updated June 1996. Available at www.ama-assn.org.

Benson Machine Company
Dealing with a Client's Large Ego

LISTEN TO ME!" Rick Benson told Jack Aaron, president of Ace Design, over the telephone. "Here's exactly what I want Ace Design to do. I want to see several more designs for our new corporate identity graphics that are abstract, colorful, and creative. Maybe use the elements in some nontraditional way. So far, all I have seen are recommendations based on the use of a stylized B for Benson Machine Company, and I hate them all. Using a letter as part of a logo is 1970s thinking."

"Rick, up to this point we have been in agreement on the creative direction," Jack replied. "Two weeks ago we showed you an abstract design and a whole array of nontraditional approaches. But you indicated you didn't want us to pursue any of those further, and you instructed us to concentrate on a 'more traditional approach.' This is what we have done. We can go back and start again with additional alternatives. But that will take time, and the more hours we invest in this project, the higher the cost. I have looked at where your budget is to date, and to do what you are requesting will require more money than you originally approved."

Jack waited for a response, but there was none. Then he heard the phone go dead. Apparently Rick wasn't pleased with Jack's observation that to do what Rick wanted would cost more money.

THE PRICING POLICY AT ACE DESIGN

Ever since its founding in 1998, Ace Design has followed a standard procedure when called on to do a job. Each designer prepares his or her own formalized estimates that are then presented to the client for approval. The estimates contain the designer's best assessment of the time it will take to do the job, and it also lists any "outside" costs that might be incurred, such as paying for photography, printing, or supplies.

Like most design firms and ad agencies, Ace charges its clients based on the time it takes to do a job. Each task performed by the designer carries an hourly rate, from concept, to art direction, to layout, to the actual creation of the artwork on a disc that a printer or magazine will use to print the piece. Rates range from $75 to $125 per hour. If the total cost of the time put into the average job is divided by the hours it took, a "blended rate" (or average rate) for all tasks and services is about $95 per hour.

In preparing an estimate, a designer needs to allow enough hours to get the job done profitably. On the other hand, building in too much of a cushion to cover the unexpected can result in pricing that is out of line or not competitive. Probably the best way to estimate a job is to find a past job that is similar and see how much time was involved. But this is only a starting point. Different designers work at different paces, have varying computer skills, and differ in how quickly they can come to a creative solution. So it is very possible that if a design company assigned the identical job to each of its designers, there could be as many different estimates as there are designers (although they would probably all be close).

Experience has shown that providing the estimated cost is only part of a good estimate. The management of Ace requires that all of its designers very carefully include, in detail, just what the estimate covers. (Figure 26.1 shows the estimate prepared for and approved by Rick Benson.) Preparing an estimate requires asking a number of questions, such as the following:

- Is there a need for copywriting?
- In what form will the initial work be shown to the client (rough sketches or computer generated)?
- How many revisions are included in the estimate?
- How many meetings with the client?
- Is production beyond creation of the artwork included?
- What about photography, shipping, tax, . . . etc.?

RICK BENSON

At six feet five inches tall, Rick Benson was an imposing presence. As president and founder of Benson Machine Company, Rick had guided his company to almost 25 years of growth and profitability. Benson Machine had numerous competitors locally, nationally, and internationally. Operating in the business-to-business marketplace, the company was often engaged in fierce bidding wars with competitors for business in the not-so-glamorous world of making machine tools. Many of the people in this business come from a blue-collar background, and often they have lived or were born in the northeast or in the area around the southern part of the Great Lakes.

FIGURE 26.1

Ace Design Estimate for Benson Machine Company

ESTIMATE

Benson Machine Company
BMC0001

Logo

Ace Design will show 2-4 initial logotype concepts in unfinished form. Working with the client, Ace Design will then narrow down the ideas to 1 or 2 directions for further development. After selecting one of these, Ace Design will provide further development.

$5,000.00

The final selected logo will be executed into its final form and produced in digital format.

Submitted By _____ Date _____

Approved By _____ Date _____

Terms: 50% of approved estimate due upon approval.
Invoices due upon receipt. Taxes and shipping not included.
All estimates are +/- 10%.

Rick's background was somewhat unusual for a president of a business-to-business company. Thirty years ago, Rick graduated from a well-known and respected university art program. For the first two years after college, Rick was an artist and designer for a small ad agency in Cleveland. His previous career as a designer, 25 years of being "the man in charge," and a quick temper made Rick not the easiest client to work with.

Now, Jack Aaron had to decide what to do. Ace had already billed Rick for 50 percent of the initial estimate, which was its policy, and Benson's check had been received. Based on the original estimate, Benson was to be billed another $2,500 upon project completion. Jack wondered, "How am I going to get Rick to pay the remaining $2,500 he owes Ace Design?" Jack also knew that Benson Machine Company could have more work for Ace Design in the future. At an earlier meeting, Rick had mentioned "a brochure, presentation materials, and a website."

Dealings with Rick were not always easy, and the next contact with Rick was likely to be testy at best.

QUESTIONS

1. When should Jack call Rick again? And what stance should Jack take? Explain your reasoning.
2. Do you think Rick will pay for the additional work he is demanding? Explain.
3. Should Ace Design just do what Rick is demanding and not bill for it? Why, or why not?
4. Should Jack ask to see Rick in person to discuss the situation? What would that meeting be like?
5. Should Jack tell anyone else at Ace Design about this situation with Benson Machine Company? Why, or why not? Whom would Jack tell?
6. Does the possibility of any future work from Benson Machine Company impact this situation, or your recommendation for what Jack should do?

E-Commerce and Pandora's Box

PANDORA'S BOX was founded two decades ago by Micah Goldman in Chicago, Illinois, after his father, who owned a women's clothing store, persuaded him to forget a career in broadcasting and think about sales. Pandora's Box was located in an exclusive neighborhood and offered the best brands of women's clothing, including expensive lingerie. The fashionable store featured items that appealed to women in their 30s, 40s, and 50s. Goldman's store became very successful. Indeed, he opened another store in an upscale mall. This store, too, became very successful, and Goldman opened another store, which was also successful.

Although Goldman hired an advertising agency to develop advertising campaigns for his company, journalists and feature writers wrote stories and articles about the business. Most of these reports focused on the unusual interior designs and colors of each store, which women, when interviewed, said they appreciated. Women also pointed out that they liked shopping at the stores because each one had a coffee shop that featured international coffees and other drinks as well as chocolates and desserts from all over the world.

Goldman expanded his company shortly after the World Wide Web became popular. He had a colorful website developed that featured lingerie. Pandora's Box Direct allowed shoppers to order any undergarment offered by the company from the privacy of their home. Online prices were very competitive, because shoppers had to pay a fee for shipping and handling. The first year's sales from the company's website were $2.5 million, which was more than Goldman had anticipated. Although he had worried that online sales might decrease his stores' sales, this was not the case. Indeed, his stores' sales had increased more than 10 percent the same year. The second year's sales from the online business were $3.25 million. Goldman's company (stores and online) continued to grow. In addition to offering lingerie online, the company started offering several private-label brands of higher-priced fragrances. These fragrances were sold exclusively at Pandora's Box.

THE CASE

Melanie Turney, president of Pandora's Box Direct, looked at the statistics again: fewer than 50 percent of their online customers had purchased any of their higher-priced fragrances. Yet, Turney realized, the company had an opportunity to continue to be one of the best and most profitable by providing higher-priced fragrances to online customers. The division could further grow sales and capture a greater share of the market. She thought that if the company marketed its fragrances aggressively to its online customers, these customers would remember the brands, which would lead to further sales. Several brands had become best sellers in the stores, and Turney realized that the division had not done enough as far as advertising the brands to customers who shopped at the website.

She looked at the plan that the marketing department had developed. In it, the marketing director and others discussed the advertising they thought was needed to aggressively market Pandora's Box's higher-priced fragrances to their online customers. They had included a direct mail piece that would be sent to every customer who ordered online, an e-mail attachment that would be sent to every customer who ordered online, and an in-store display to remind those customers who also ordered online.

The direct mail piece included a visually appealing announcement about Pandora's Box's higher-priced fragrances, along with a 25 percent off coupon on one order that totaled at least $50. The e-mail attachment included the same piece as the direct mail— the visually appealing announcement and the 25 percent off coupon. The in-store display, which would be placed in every Pandora's Box, announced the Pandora's Box higher-priced fragrances and included a supply of the 25 percent off coupons that could be used online.

QUESTIONS

1. Do you think the marketing department's advertising plan will reach Pandora's Box customers, especially those who order online? Why? Why not?
2. Do you think the direct mail piece is appropriate and relevant to advertising Pandora's Box's higher-priced fragrances? Why? Why not?
3. Do you think the e-mail attachment is appropriate and relevant to advertising Pandora's Box's higher-priced fragrances? Why? Why not?
4. Do you think the in-store display is appropriate and relevant to advertising Pandora's Box's higher-priced fragrances? Why? Why not?

5. Do you think the advertising plan will increase awareness and sales of Pandora's Box's higher-priced fragrances? Why? Why not?

6. If you were hired by Turney as a consultant, what would you advise her to include in the advertising plan that would reach Pandora's Box customers, especially those who order online, and increase awareness and sales of the company's higher-priced fragrances? Why?

7. Considering the facts in the case, do you think Pandora's Box's higher-priced fragrances are the products that should be advertised now by the company? Why? Why not?

8. When developing the advertising plan, does the marketing department need to consider other variables besides the fact that fewer than 50 percent of their online customers had purchased the higher-priced fragrances? Or do you think this is the target market that should be addressed with advertising? Explain your reasoning.

Advertising a Recording Artist
Using Short Message Service (SMS) and Multimedia Messaging Service (MMS)

NUMEROUS COMPANIES are having agencies and other firms develop advertising campaigns that employ text messaging and other forms of advertising, including commercials that can be received by cell phones. Text messaging is referred to as short message service (SMS). A message that contains visual elements and sound is referred to as multimedia messaging service (MMS). Cellular phones can receive text messages that contain information, including advertising, from businesses. One reason text messaging is increasing in popularity is that it can deliver advertisements to individuals who are members of a target market. A target market's size (number of individuals) can vary from a few to millions. And the messages can be delivered quickly. However, in order for text message and other forms of advertising to be effective, they must be relatively brief. The advertisement must get to the point.

Mobile marketing is being used by companies large and small. The Discovery Channel, for instance, for its program *I Shouldn't Be Alive*, offered free ringtones and weekly trivia questions to cell-phone subscribers. *American Idol*, a popular program on the Fox network, has encouraged individuals to vote for contestants via text messaging. ESPN has offered news, videos of sportscasts, and scores of athletic competitions using this medium. Other companies use text messaging to inform customers about their products or special sales, or both.

However, studies have indicated that consumers are not necessarily interested in receiving advertising, especially if they did not ask for it.[1] Nonetheless, according to Thomas J. Burgess of Third Screen Media, advertisers are interested in cell phones because customers click on the banner advertisements. Indeed, the click-through rate is 4 percent on cell phones; it is only 1 percent on the Internet.[2] According to Enpocket, a company that helps advertisers send their messages via cell phones, 15 percent of users respond to text-message advertisements, which is twice the percentage of those who respond to direct mail advertisements.[3]

Although companies are not spending fortunes on advertising in this medium, some professionals believe that this will change as the medium develops. What will cell phones be like in one or two years in terms of screen size and better graphics? Some observers think that companies will invest considerably more dollars on advertising in this medium in the not too distant future. For instance, John Stratton, chief marketing officer at Verizon Wireless, believes mobile advertising will account for 25 percent to 30 percent of the $100 billion spent on branding in the United States each year over the next few years.[4]

THE CASE

Several executives of R 'n' R Records, a popular label that was founded by a young, innovative musician-turned-businessman, were seated at a large table in a conference room. They were meeting with J. J. Thompson, the founder of a relatively new company that had integrated SMS and MMS with other media in advertising and marketing campaigns.

J. J. Thompson turned to the head of the recording company, Rick Davis, and said, "Let me ask you a few questions about your industry before I tell you what my company can do for you. Okay?"

Rick nodded and replied, "Sure."

"Why don't you explain the typical breakdown of your company. I'm curious."

Rick looked at the other two executives he had asked to attend the meeting. "Well, I am the president and CEO of the company, which has four major departments. The departments include Business Affairs, which Ben Goldberg manages—unfortunately, Ben couldn't be here. Business Affairs handles legal concerns, accounting, advances, royalties, and contracts. The International Department handles our various products abroad. Ed Carter here manages Sales and Marketing." Ed, seated next to Rick, nodded and smiled. "They take care of air play, corporate sponsorships, direct response sales, merchandising, record clubs, sales aids, touring, and video. Bill Jackson, over there, heads Creative Services." Bill nodded and waved. "They take care of our artists, from the production of their recordings to generating buzz or publicity about them and their products."

J. J. nodded and said, "Thanks. The organization sounds similar to other companies in your category that I've worked with."

"When I started the company years ago," Rick said, "the organization was nothing like it is today, believe me."

J. J. said, "That's success, Rick."

The executives laughed.

Rick said, "As you know from our conversation on the phone, Billie's new recording is ready." Billie was one of the label's new artists who had been performing in major cities throughout the Southeast. She had a loyal following. Rick had heard about her from one of the company's employees. Rick, Ed, and Bill saw her in concert last year and several days later offered her a contract.

J. J. said, "I remember, Rick. You said that Ed's department had come up with a marketing plan that included full-page ads in *Billboard* and other recording magazines, as well as a video that will be broadcast on one of the cable networks."

"That's right. The company has had a lot of success doing similar ads and videos. But last year, like other recording companies, we've seen our sales decrease. That's one reason we're here. To find out if you can come up with something that will add to what Ed's department has developed."

J. J. glanced at the executives and said, "Although you've had considerable success in using the traditional media, you have to realize that you're trying to sell an artist and her product to a much younger consumer—a consumer who doesn't necessarily use the traditional media. For instance, today we have three screens—the television, the computer, and now cell phones. Young people are using the latter much like we use the computer. More than 200 million people in the United States have cell phones. More than one-fourth of these people have used text messaging on their phones, and more than one-eighth have used the Internet on their phones. I'm sure that you're aware millions have purchased ringtones."

Rick and the other executives nodded.

"Guess what? Guess who uses text-messaging? Guess who's responding to advertising messages on cell phones? By and large, young people."

Rick and the other executives looked at each other.

J. J. stood and started pacing back and forth. "Here's what I think we need to add to what Ed's department has come up with. Have you heard of C-T-I-A?"

Rick nodded. "I've heard of it."

"Well, C-T-I-A, which is an association for wireless, issues short codes for a fee. The fee varies depending on how long a company wants to use it. When a consumer punches in the code, the code goes into a queue. In short, an operator does not have to answer phone calls. If a message needs to be returned, it's sent to a caller's phone as text; the caller can retrieve it at his or her leisure."

Ed said, "I receive text messages, but I didn't know the process behind them. Interesting."

J. J. said, "I think a code should be published in the print ad and superimposed at the end of the video. This will allow fans to punch in the code on their cell phones and get textual messages about Billie's new CD as well as about when and where she will perform. Other messages will inform them about ordering tickets. We can offer the video at Billie's website or the company's website. We can even ask fans in a text message if they want to receive parts of the video on their cell phones. I think we can influence fans to purchase the product and concert tickets this way. If it's not too late, you need to publish a code on the CD's package. This can be a small paste-on label with instructions that tell consumers to punch in the code on their cell phones. If they do this, they possibly will win tickets to one of the artist's concerts, or a downloadable coupon that can be used to purchase the artist's tickets at a reduced price. Of course, we could sell additional products, too, such as individual songs, via their cell phones."

J. J. looked at Rick. "Rick, what do you think?"

Rick looked at J. J. and smiled. He liked the ideas, but he wondered if they needed to do all that J. J. suggested. He also wondered how expensive the ideas, if implemented, would be.

QUESTIONS

1. What do you think Rick will do? Explain.
2. What would you do? Explain.
3. What if Rick chose one or two of the ideas that J. J. mentioned. Which one or two ideas do you think he should employ? Why? You may wish to read more about mobile marketing before you try answering this question.
4. What if Rick learns that the ideas he's selected will add more than $50,000 to the already expensive marketing plan for Billie's CD. Do you think he will tell J. J. to go ahead? Why?
5. What if Rick wants to employ one or more of J. J.'s ideas, but Ed doesn't. Do you think Rick should make the decision—after all, he's the president and CEO? Or do you think he should listen to Ed—after all, Ed's in charge of the Sales and Marketing Department? Explain your reasoning.
6. Do you think mobile marketing can help sell recording artists and their products, including concerts? Why? Why not? Support your answer with statistical data, or at least an article that discusses the positives versus the negatives about this subject and recording artists and their products.

NOTES

1. Paul Korzeniowski, "Cell Phones Emerge as New Advertising Medium," *TechNewsWorld*, November 16, 2005. Available at www.technewsworld.com.

2. Matt Richtel, "Marketers Interested in Small Screen," *New York Times*, January 16, 2006. Available at www.nytimes.com.

3. Korzeniowski, "Cell Phones Emerge as New Advertising Medium."

4. Olga Kharif, "Now Playing on Your Cell Phone: Advertisers Are Jumping on the Mobile Marketing Bandwagon. Will Subscribers Join Them?" *BusinessWeek* Online, March 24, 2006. Available at http://web.lexis-nexis.com.

The Communications Plan of the First National Bank of Kettering

BERNARD SIMS, the president of the First National Bank, Kettering, Ohio, said hello to the assembled executives before he sat down at the conference table. "I'm sorry, Rebecca, for being late. I just got out of a meeting with the board of directors."

Rebecca Heffinberg was the bank's marketing director; she had been hired a year before and had been doing excellent work, according to more than one of the bank's vice presidents. Rebecca stood at the end of the table, in front of a screen, holding a report. She said, "I've placed copies of my complete report on the table in front of you, and I'll show you some of the highlights on the screen. First, I'd like to draw your attention to our consumer survey, which was conducted by the Target Market Research Company. It begins on the second page of the report. As you can see, we asked some 5,000 people several questions pertaining to banking. The majority, or 73 percent, said they were happy where they banked. However, most, or 65 percent, said they did not know what their banks offered, other than the basics such as checking accounts, savings accounts, and loans for cars, houses, and the like. When the interviewer informed them about our bank and what we offered, 67 percent of the respondents were surprised."

Sims said, "Interesting. Apparently, we haven't done a very good job in getting the word out about what we provide."

Rebecca nodded. "You're right. Just look at the next figure. As you can see, 77 percent of the respondents did not remember seeing any information about our bank. Yet we had been advertising for several months prior to the survey. On the other hand, 79 percent remembered reading or hearing about Roger Morris, the manager at one of the branches in Dayton who died of a heart attack on his way to work. Now, let's look at some data

TABLE 29.1
Population of Kettering, Ohio

Total Population—57,502
Male—20,692 (18 and older)
Female—23,871 (18 and older)

AGE	NUMBER OF PERSONS	PERCENTAGE OF POPULATION
18 YEARS AND OVER	44,563	77.5
18 to 19 years	1,180	2.6
20 to 24 years	3,157	5.5
25 to 34 years	8,173	14.2
35 to 44 years	8,746	15.2
45 to 54 years	7,512	13.1
55 to 59 years	2,817	4.9
60 to 64 years	2,480	4.3
65 to 74 years	5,344	9.3
75 to 84 years	4,021	7.0
85 years and over	1,133	2.0

Median age (years)—38.9

about Kettering." Rebecca drew their attention to the screen, which showed the information depicted in table 29.1.

"As you can see, I've broken down the population by age ranges, starting at 18 and going to 85-plus," Rebecca said. She gave them time to look at the statistics before going on. Then she changed the screen to the material shown in table 29.2.

"Although the city's population is 57,502, almost 55,000 are white. Only 900-plus are African Americans, only 800-plus are Hispanic, and only 700-plus are Asians," she said.

Rebecca then moved on to the information depicted in table 29.3. "As you can see, there are almost 16,000 family households. More than 12,000 are headed by married couples, while more than 2,000 are headed by females only. There are almost 10,000 nonfamily households."

The image on the screen changed again. "As you see, the next table shows housing occupancy for Kettering." Rebecca indicated the material depicted in table 29.4.

"Rebecca, what is the value of the average house in Kettering? Do you know?" Sims asked.

"Yes. It's $111,000. However, last year, there were 30 new houses built; the average cost was $164,500."

TABLE 29.2

Population of Kettering by Race

	NUMBER OF PERSONS	PERCENTAGE OF POPULATION
Caucasian	54,757	95.2
African American	955	1.7
Asian	795	1.4
Hispanic	806	1.4
Other	189	0.3

TABLE 29.3

Kettering, Ohio, Households by Type

Total Households—25,657
Average Household Size—2.22
Average Family Size—2.85

	NUMBER OF PERSONS	PERCENTAGE OF POPULATION
Family households	15,715	61.3
Married-couple family	12,506	48.7
Headed by female only	2,446	9.5
Nonfamily households	9,942	38.7
Householder living alone	8,561	33.4
Householder 65 years or older	3,256	12.7

Rebecca moved on to information about the education levels of the population, as shown in table 29.5.

"Of the population 25 years and over, almost 11,000 have a high school diploma. Almost 10,000 have attended college. More than 3,000 have at least an associate's degree, almost 8,000 have a bachelor's degree, and more than 4,500 people have a graduate or professional degree. In short, 91 percent have finished high school, and 31 percent have finished college. Compared to many cities of its size, Kettering has a more highly educated population. Kettering also enjoys a low unemployment rate; only 2.2 percent. Many work in management, professions, sales, or related occupations. The average family's income is almost $56,000 a year."

"So what does all of this mean?" Sims asked.

"It means, first, that people are not learning about us through our advertising. Second, Kettering's people are highly educated, with good jobs. Third, primarily because of the average family's high income, these people need our services. For instance, just consider the number of students from this community who attend colleges and univer-

TABLE 29.4

Housing Occupancy, Kettering, Ohio

Total Housing Units—26,936

TYPE OF UNIT	NUMBER OF UNITS	PERCENTAGE OF TOTAL UNITS
Occupied Housing Units	25,657	95.3
Vacant Housing Units	1,279	4.7
Owner-occupied Housing Units	17,088	66.6
Renter-occupied Housing Units	8,569	33.4

TABLE 29.5

Education Levels of the Kettering Population

Population 25 Years and Over—40,226

HIGHEST LEVEL COMPLETED	NUMBER OF PERSONS	PERCENTAGE OF TOTAL
High school graduate	10,755	26.8
Some college, no degree	9,923	24.7
Associate degree	3,411	8.5
Bachelor's degree	7,925	19.7
Graduate or professional degree	4,533	11.3

sities that are here or near here. Many of these students or their parents need our services, such as education loans. Yet, as Dave Gregarian can tell you, the number of education loans is down this year."

Dave Gregarian, who headed the loan department and was seated near Sims, nodded. "What do you propose we do?" Sims asked.

"I'm proposing that we cut back on advertising in the traditional media and focus on promotion and public relations," Rebecca replied. She changed the screen image to a list with bullet points. "Specifically, I'm proposing that we cut our advertising in half. I think we should rent only two outdoor displays, place only one ad each week in the paper—preferably Sunday—and run fewer spots on television. I think we need to start advertising on the World Wide Web, specifically on websites that are for car dealerships and real estate companies. We should also expand our website. And we need to heavy up our promotion efforts. We need to get our name before the public wherever large groups gather, such as sporting events, especially children's sporting events. Although I have some ideas about how and where to do this, I'm still working on the specific promotional tools, events, and dates. This holds true for the public relations tools and dates, too."

QUESTIONS

1. Based on the information in the case, specifically the demographics of who lives in Kettering, do you think Rebecca's decision about cutting advertising in the traditional media makes sense? Why, or why not? (Remember: people who are more affluent and well educated tend to read print media more often.)

2. Do you think her idea about advertising on the Web is sound? Why? Why not?

3. Based on the information in the case, what promotional activities do you think the bank should employ? Why? (You may wish to learn more about promotional activities before you answer this question.)

4. What public relations communications tools do you think the bank should employ? Why? (You may wish to learn more about public relations communications tools before you answer this question.)

5. Let's say that Rebecca's marketing budget is $100,000 a year. Identify the media, promotional activities, and public relations communications tools she should use, and how much she should spend on each to reach the major target market. You will need to identify the target market: think about those who will benefit the most from the bank's services. Provide a reason for each medium and the expenditures for it.

6. Develop a media schedule for the entire year that Rebecca can use.

Teaching a Client about Advertising Design

JOHN ROBERTS has been a member of the advertising staff at the *Daily Herald*, a medium-size daily newspaper, for several years. He is responsible for selling advertising space and writing and designing advertisements for several clients who advertise in the newspaper several times a week. However, he is having a difficult time with a new client, Alison Harvey, who started a successful small business—a clothing boutique for women—but is not very informed about newspapers or advertising.

John spent considerable time on more than one occasion with this client, but now he is getting perturbed at having to provide reasons for the headlines, subheads, body copy, and artwork in the client's advertisements. Yet the client insists on being informed as to why John is using this headline or that headline, this subhead or that subhead, this block of copy or that block of copy, this piece of artwork or that piece of artwork. She also usually grills him about the overall design.

John had just finished a half-page advertisement for the client when she walked in and asked to see it. John handed the piece to her. She examined it closely, then she said, "Do you think this headline is the best headline for the items I'm selling?"

John nodded and replied, "Yes, I do. Otherwise, I wouldn't have written it."

Alison Harvey sensed tension in the air, but she pressed on. "What about the subheads? I don't like this one." She pointed at the second subhead, which introduced women's blouses.

"What's wrong with it?" John asked.

"I don't like how it sounds."

"Can you be more specific?"

"I don't like the words you've chosen. They sound too masculine."

"Ms. Harvey, there's nothing wrong with the subhead. The words are not 'too masculine.'"

"Still, I don't like it. Change it."

"Okay. Anything else while you're here?"

"Yes. I don't like the design. What if you moved the large photograph here?" She pointed to the top of the advertisement.

"Well, if I did what you're suggesting, the advertisement would be lopsided. There would be too much weight at the top and not enough at the bottom. Not only that, the dominant photograph would be too far from the optical center."

"Huh?"

"Look, Ms. Harvey, you'll have to trust me."

"Oh, okay, but change that subhead."

"Of course."

"And let me know what you change it to before you run it. Okay?"

"Okay, Ms. Harvey."

John watched her leave. Then he looked at the advertisement and shook his head. "There's nothing wrong with that subhead," he said aloud. He decided to find Bob Turner, the advertising manager.

Bob was talking to Charlotte Johnson, another advertising staff member.

"Take a look at this advertisement and tell me what you think," John said to them.

Bob examined the advertisement. "John, this is excellent." He handed the advertisement to Charlotte.

Charlotte looked at the advertisement. "John, this is great. I don't see one thing that needs changing."

"Well, tell that to the client, Alison Harvey. She was here a few minutes ago and told me to change this subhead. She said it sounded too masculine."

"You must be joking," Charlotte said.

John shook his head. "I'm not joking."

"Did she have any suggestions?" Bob asked.

"No. She just said it sounded too masculine. What do you think I should do?"

"Change it; she's paying for it," Bob replied.

"Bob, she's becoming a major pain. She has to approve every advertisement before it runs in the paper. And so far, she's requested at least one or two changes in every ad that I've created for her."

"Sounds like she's taking a lot of your time," Charlotte said.

John nodded.

Bob patted him on the back. "John, change the subhead in the ad, inform her about it, then ask her to come in for a meeting. I think we need to sit down with her and explain that we don't have time to teach every client about how to create newspaper ads. Besides, it states in her contract, like all of our contracts, that we will go over the first five ads, not any after the first five. Correct?"

"Correct."

As John changed the advertisement, he thought about what he would say to Alison Harvey. He also thought about the meeting. He decided to let Bob lead the meeting. But he realized that Bob had never met the client, so Bob was not aware of her abrasive personality. What if Bob said the wrong thing? John wondered if he should tell Bob about the client's temperament. He dismissed the idea because he realized that Bob was a professional. He'd been around a long time; he'd be able to figure her out.

Suddenly John wondered if a meeting was a good idea. The client might feel threatened. What if she stopped advertising in the paper? Her half-page advertisements ran three or four times a week. That's several thousand dollars. John wondered if he should speak to Bob again.

QUESTIONS

1. Should John and Bob meet with Alison Harvey? Why, or why not?
2. Let's say John and Bob meet with Alison Harvey. What should they say to her? Why?
3. Should newspaper advertising staff members have to meet with clients? Why, or why not?
4. Do you think clients have the right to examine every advertisement that is created for them by newspaper advertising staff members? Explain.
5. Should newspaper advertising staff members expect to have to teach clients about newspaper advertisements? Why, or why not?
6. What if Alison Harvey decides to stop advertising in the *Daily Herald*? Will Bob's job be threatened? Will John's job be threatened?
7. Do you think a newspaper should conduct a seminar for clients and potential clients about newspaper advertising? Explain.

PART IV

The Ad Agency

Norman Surgical Supply Company, LLC
An Owner's Mindset

ONE OF THE most fundamental "we/they" distinctions in the business world is that of "owners" and "employees." Many people work for publicly traded companies while they own stock in that same company. So, actually, they are owners and employees at the same time. But in the small-business world, the majority of employees are not owners of the company they work for. However, the owner or owners may well be employees. This is the case with Norman Surgical Supply Company, LLC.

Charles Norman founded the company in 1993, using savings and a second mortgage on his home for the initial capitalization. Joining him in the initial setup were three partners: Drew Cass, Amy Young, and Linda Meyers. Owners of a limited liability company (LLC) are known as "members," and the operating agreement prepared by the company's attorney assigned 45 percent of the membership shares (the company stock) to Charles, 25 percent to Drew, 20 percent to Amy, and 10 percent to Linda. This assignment was in proportion to the amount of cash that each of them contributed to the initial capitalization when the company was started.

Member	Capital Contribution	% Ownership
Charles Norman	$90,000	45%
Drew Cass	$40,000	25%
Amy Young	$40,000	20%
Linda Meyers	$30,000	10%

The operating agreement, drafted by a law firm that specialized in setting up LLCs, required majority approval for any expenditure in excess of $1,500. This meant that even though Charles Norman was the president, he needed to have at least one other person agree with his purchase decisions, because Charles held only 45 percent of the shares. The addition of anyone else's "yes" would mean that owners with more than 50 percent of the shares were in agreement. If the other three owners disagreed with Charles's spending plans for goods or services in excess of $1,500, then they could veto his decision because together they held 55 percent of the stock.

Norman Surgical Supply had grown since 1993 and now had 42 employees. Among them were Charles, the company president; Drew, the chief marketing officer; Amy, director of operations; and Linda, the chief financial officer. Drew had worked for several other companies but had never been a company owner either solely or in part. As a result, it took him some time to fully understand and adjust to his new role.

One day, while getting gas for his new car, he overheard two young adults admiring his car. The first said, "He probably *owns* a company," while the second said, "I wish *I* owned a company."

This got Drew thinking. Did these two people understand what company ownership means? Clearly, the assumption was that being an owner meant that you could afford an expensive car. The comments seemed to reflect an assumption of owner prerogative. But did they also represent a statement of class status as well? Was this a widely held set of beliefs in the workplace or just the random comments of two young people? Or was there really something different about the way small-business owners think and the way the average non-owner thinks about working, business in general, responsibility, workplace behavior, and compensation?

That same evening, after dinner, Drew decided to make a list of questions related to the above issues. Next week, Drew would pose this list of questions to the advertising management class he taught on Tuesday nights at a local university. And, while these questions wouldn't deal with advertising management per se, they would deal with issues that many of his students would face in the future as owners, employees, or both.

QUESTIONS

Here is Drew's list of questions. Answer each one, and provide the reasoning for your answers.

1. Should an owner in a small business think differently about the company than an average employee of the same company?
2. What are the most important things an owner should be concerned about?
3. Should all the owners in a company take part in the company's management?
4. Should company owners make more money than the employees?

5. What are the potential financial benefits of business ownership?
6. How open should the owners be with the employees about the company's financial situation? How about other company information?
7. What benefits should owners provide to employees?
8. What does the "Right to Work" law mean? Is the state where your college or university is located a "Right to Work State"?
9. What does "thinking like an owner" mean?

Polk, Fales & Crumley Advertising
When an Agency Becomes Stale

THE CLASSIC AD agency compensation model was built around the expectation of 15 percent commission on media placed by the agency for its clients. For many years, this accepted methodology was accepted by all media, ad agencies, and clients. Beginning in the 1970s, however, clients started to ask, "Why a 15 percent commission?" Many national advertisers such as GM, IBM, and Coca-Cola, each of which spent hundreds of millions of dollars annually, began to first ask, then tell, their agencies that they intended to pay only a 12.5 percent commission. Then, just a 10 percent commission. And finally, most national and regional advertisers started to ask ad agencies, "How *little* will you charge me to place my media?" Competition led to agencies making deals that were good for clients, but often not so good for the agencies.

This awareness that a client did not *have* to pay a fixed media commission, and that all commissions were negotiable, led even local advertisers dealing with small ad agencies to demand a more favorable media commission structure, or even no commission at all. In the rush to get new clients, many ad agencies of all sizes made deals with their clients on media commissions that came back to haunt them later. Since media commissions were the primary source of agency income through the 1970s, the amount of money agencies made from creating and placing a client's advertising diminished sharply.

Since ad agencies are in business to make money for owners and employees, agencies had to find other ways to generate income, other than from media commissions. Some ad agencies figured it out immediately, while some agencies never did. One of the ad agencies that took longer than others to figure it out was Polk, Fales & Crumley.

POLK, FALES & CRUMLEY ADVERTISING

Three very talented people founded Polk, Fales & Crumley Advertising, or PF&C: John Polk, David Fales, and Betsy Crumley. John was the president and account guy, David was the creative talent, and Betsy was the business brain. Early in their agency's life they had been very fortunate to have several accounts that were media intensive. This meant that they had become accustomed to the 15 percent media commissions that agencies enjoyed from the media they placed, and this was a large part of their income.

As successive PF&C clients negotiated less than full 15 percent media commissions, the amount of income the agency generated for a given amount of work decreased. Betsy was reluctant to move to the all-fee-based system of compensation that John Polk favored. Creative Director David Fales had no opinion on the matter; his creative department was doing "great work," and the economics of running an agency were of secondary importance to him. But as agency media commissions declined, gross income suffered. Since gross income is what agencies use to pay such expenses as salaries and rent, the agency had to rein in spending. This caused chief financial officer Betsy Crumley to watch costs very closely every month.

John Polk still intended to institute an all-fee-based compensation system. But with Betsy not committed to it, and David not really interested, John did not have the commitments he needed among the other owners to make such a sweeping change. He needed more time to convince the other two owners.

WHILE THE CLOCK IS TICKING

An ad agency's mood is a fragile thing. When an agency is rapidly winning new business pitches and acquiring new accounts, the mood can be euphoric and giddy. Immediately, everyone sees salary increases and bigger bonuses. People start talking about the need for additional staff, and generally someone will mention that "we might as well start looking for larger space." This same sense of pride and achievement occurs when agencies win creative awards. What better validation of your talent is there than to have peers recognize it for you? Cabinets and display cases get built to show off awards, press releases fly to local and national media, and everyone starts to think about salary increases and bigger bonuses.

While this positive momentum is absolutely exhilarating to be around, negative momentum can have a similarly dramatic impact in the other direction. And it doesn't take much to change an agency's mood. The daily intradepartmental interactions required to make an agency run smoothly can easily lead to a platform on which staff dissatisfaction is verbalized and spread.

This negative mood was the situation at PF&C. Initially brought about by the need to watch expenses carefully since gross income was declining from reduced media commissions, it was further fueled by a couple of layoffs, the loss of a longtime client, and overall frustration because it appeared that the owners were not addressing the core problem.

THE TRICKLE-DOWN THEORY
OF NEGATIVE MOOD

Often, when things are not going well at an ad agency, the most obvious reflection of this is seen in the creative department. Creative people generally want to have more than adequate resources to do "great work." This means budgets large enough to hire the best photographers, illustrators, and production people. When expenses are being carefully watched, the creative staff may believe they are not getting the resources they need to do "great work." The perception of restricted resources, rather than the actuality, is often enough to get a creative department off their game and complaining about work that "could have been better if there was more money."

This thinking can lead to average creative work: "We don't have the money to be great!" It can also result in missed deadlines due to indifference, and to a general malaise. It leads to creative solutions that are ordinary or not inspired. The client sees this as unimaginative, "stale" creative work.

The next department usually affected by a general malaise at an agency is the account service group. These individuals are the primary client contact. When agency gross income is down, and expenses are being carefully watched, there is a reluctance to "entertain," meaning that clients are not taken to lunch or ball games or invited to play golf. While on the surface this might seem "frivolous," relationship building with clients through entertainment has been a part of agency–client relations since the very first ad agency. Without professional trust built from social interactions, account people become "vendors" and clients become "buyers." In this environment, it becomes difficult for account service people to casually "pitch ideas" to their clients, or for account people to work overtime on trying to build a client's business. When account people stop bringing new ideas to clients, or are perceived as no longer trying to help a client build his or her business, the agency is viewed as stale.

An agency media department lives off of the interaction it has with the agency's creative and account service departments. Together, the account executive and the media planner make recommendations to the client regarding the best media to use to reach the target audience. If a malaise has set in, media people often don't get cooperation from the creative people regarding their thoughts on which creative materials or sizes will work best (half-page or full-page; color or black and white; television, radio, or outdoor advertising). If the media people start questioning the possible effectiveness of recommended creative executions, or if they think the creative people are defaulting to traditional media when nontraditional media would be more effective, the media planners and buyers might just go through the motions of planning and buying media that they don't believe in. If they do this, and if they don't (or can't) show the client some creative and outside-the-box thinking regarding media selection, then the agency can be viewed as stale.

This same staleness can manifest itself in any research done by the agency, or in public relations or other areas, such as promotions or trade relations. Often it doesn't take much for an entire agency to drift into the malaise. And agency management is not immune from being seen as stale by a client. It can occur because of observed attitudes, judgments about a manager's age, or just plain fatigue at the top. But it is the responsibility of agency management to keep employees active, challenged, and motivated.

SYMPTOMS OF A STALE AD AGENCY

At the annual planning meeting with the four representatives of the Toddy Company, a major client, PF&C presented a new advertising campaign and related materials, a new media plan, and its best thinking on how to help Toddy build its business for the coming year. The PF&C presenters were well dressed, well prepared, and well rehearsed. They managed to finish earlier than the two hours they had said it would take to discuss such important matters. All of the visual aids, charts, PowerPoint presentations, and audio equipment functioned as they were supposed to. And lunch, which was prepared by one of the best caterers in town, was superb.

After the Toddy group left, there was a somewhat unenthusiastic round of self-congratulations among the PF&C staffers who were present. Yet no one really thought the agency had done that great a job. But maybe the Toddy people weren't paying that much attention. Everything was probably going to be fine. PF&C's long relationship with the Toddy Company would probably pull them through. After all, it had in the past.

THE CLIENT'S VIEW

As the Toddy group drove back to their company, there was a surprising initial silence. Each seemed to be thinking about what he or she had just heard and seen. The first to speak was the sales manager. "I wish they had addressed our deteriorating sales situation in Tampa."

Next, the merchandising director said, "I thought they were going to show us new packaging and talk about some of the new and innovative in-store displays that they mentioned six weeks ago."

As the comments started to come, Administrative Assistant Donna Cook made the following notes:

The creative seemed "uninspired."
The media planner looked bored.
No new ideas.
NO PASSION, FIRE, OR ENTHUSIASM!
Same media plan as last year; nothing new.
Broadband? Blogs? Daytime TV? Who reads newspapers?
They were surprised by what WE SAID our competition was doing!
Presentation: B+; content: C.

As the group arrived back at their office, Senior Vice President of Marketing Ken Morrison greeted them. "How was the meeting?"

"Kind of disappointing, actually," said the sales manager.

"Tell me what happened," Ken replied.

With that, the group retired to a nearby conference room and began discussing what the agency had recommended for the coming year. As Ken listened, he began to wonder what he should do. Clearly, his group was uninspired by the meeting at PF&C. Was the ad agency getting stale?

QUESTIONS

1. Is there a difference between a "bad performance" by an ad agency and a "bad agency"? Explain.
2. Can an agency recover from a bad performance? Why, or why not?
3. What does having a "stale" ad agency mean?
4. What should Ken Morrison do? What should PF&C do?
5. What should a client expect from its ad agency?
6. How closely should agency compensation drive its performance?
7. Can an advertising agency be great creatively but stale in other areas?
8. What role should an advertising agency play with its clients?
9. Is there still a role for an advertising agency in today's world?

P-O-P Advertising and the Taylor Advertising Agency

S ARAH WARNER, a junior account executive for the Taylor Advertising Agency, squirmed in her chair when she heard Jeff Taylor's comments about the agency's current advertising campaign for one of the firm's clients, a confectioner of chocolates. Jeff was her mentor, and she didn't like to doubt him, but she wasn't sold on the idea of the P-O-P displays that he was about to bring up.

"In addition to the TV spots that I've gone over," Jeff said, "we will include point-of-purchase displays that will hold 100 10-ounce bars of your company's best-selling brand, which is not selling as well as Hershey's or Nestle's best-selling brands. We intend to have your company's sales representatives try to persuade grocery store managers to display the P-O-Ps in the top 100 markets in the United States. We will have our sister agency in London do the same to try to stimulate sales in England."

Mary Richards, marketing director for the confectioner, said, "Although I liked the first part of your presentation, particularly the ideas for the 30-second TV spots, I'm wondering about the P-O-P displays."

"What are you *wondering*, Mary?" Jeff asked. Normally, he would not address a representative of a client by his or her first name, but Mary had insisted on this when they first met two years before, when the client had moved its candy bar account to Taylor's agency.

"Well, I just read where Tesco and other companies in England will no longer accept traditional P-O-P displays," Mary said. "They have more success with their in-store TV service, which allows advertisers to run advertisements. According to the article I read, Tesco claims that trials of its in-store TV service increased its advertisers' brand sales an average of 10 percent. If Tesco and other companies do this in England, how long do you think it will take for the idea to catch on in companies in the United States?"

Jeff swallowed and glanced at Sarah before he said, "You mean that Tesco is no longer accepting traditional P-O-P materials?"

Point-of-purchase materials include window and door signage, counter and shelf units, shelf talkers, cash-register signage, gondola (end of aisle) displays, dump bins, illuminated signage, motorized (motion) displays, interactive kiosks, overhead merchandisers (typically located above the cash register), cart advertisements, and aisle directory advertisements.

"I'm not sure," said Mary. "But by the time the P-O-P displays are ready, Tesco and other stores in England may have stopped accepting them. Of course, I can understand the reason for not wanting the displays. I was in a store the other day and almost drove my cart into one that was in the middle of an aisle."

Jeff nodded. "Well, I think we need to find out first before we dismiss the idea about using the P-O-Ps."

Mary didn't hear what Jeff said. She was thinking about the article. In-store TV is merely another step in a company's efforts to keep its stores clean. And Tesco had a reputation for maintaining consistent and clean messages across its stores. It was no surprise that the company went the extra mile to rid its stores of point-of-purchase material.

"What do you think, Mary?"

"What? I'm sorry, Jeff, I didn't hear you."

"I said that I think we need to find out first before we dismiss the idea about using the P-O-P displays for your chocolate bars."

Mary nodded. "Okay, but I think you need to come up with something else, just in case."

"All right." Jeff looked at the large calendar that was hanging on the wall. "Let's meet here at one o'clock next Wednesday. That should give us enough time to find out. Okay?"

Mary checked her planner. "Next Wednesday at one is fine."

"Good. We'll see you next week then."

Mary stood and walked to the door.

"Mary?"

She looked at Jeff. "Yes?"

"I promise that we'll have another idea, just in case Tesco and the other grocers are no longer accepting P-O-P displays. Okay?"

"Good!" Mary smiled at them and left.

Jeff turned to Sarah. "Sarah, I'd like you to e-mail our sister agency in London. Ask them to call the companies and find out if they intend to stop accepting P-O-P displays."

Later that day Sarah learned that Tesco was moving as quickly as possible to eliminate traditional P-O-P materials from its stores' aisles. She learned that other companies, such as Safeway, were following Tesco's lead. When she reported back to Jeff, he sighed and said, "Sarah, please instruct the creative director that his team has to come up with another idea. Explain why."

The following Wednesday, Mary, Jeff, and Sarah met again in the conference room at the agency. Jeff stood at one end of the conference table, facing Mary. "Tesco and several other companies in England intend to stop accepting P-O-P displays as soon as possible," he told her. "These companies will eliminate what has taken companies like ours, and yours, years to improve: eye-catching P-O-P material."

"I understand what you're saying, Jeff," Mary replied, "but I also understand why companies like Tesco are getting rid of displays. For years, I have shopped in stores that have displays cluttering the aisles. I think the managers of these companies are listening to their consumers."

"Mary, you know as well as I do that the retailers are partly to blame. They have allowed all sorts of P-O-P material into their stores. In other words, they do not have a consistent set of rules governing what is acceptable. Or, if they do, individual store managers have undermined the rules by altering the positions and numbers of P-O-P display stands without consulting the corporate office."

"The problem could also be that many companies are organized into departments and often these departments do not talk to one another. Sometimes, this is the problem in the company I work for," Mary said.

Jeff nodded. Mary had a point. "I understand what you're saying, but let's say, just for the sake of argument, that we can put displays of your best-selling chocolate bars into stores owned by Wal-Mart and Kroger in the top 100 markets in the United States. We must make certain that the display is designed and located to benefit both the customer and the retailer. If we forget about the latter, we will have a problem. The idea I mentioned last week considered both parties. I should point out that our idea was based on information that Incite Marketing Planning, a marketing research firm in London, learned when it conducted research for a major health and beauty brand." Turning to Sarah, Jeff asked her to give Mary an overview of the research.

"The company found that when people are shopping for something, they first try to find the leading brand—the one that they are familiar with, not necessarily the one they want," Sarah told Mary. "Once they find the leading brand, they search vertically for the one they want. So they search up and down the shelves, not across the shelves. This means that the bottom shelf is not necessarily a bad place to be. If your product is not the leading brand, it's much better to be on the shelf below or above the leader than at the end of the shelf, which contradicts what we used to believe. We used to think that a product should be as far away as possible from the leading brand. Well, that's not necessarily the case."

"Are you saying that when the P-O-P displays are ready, our sales representatives should ask the store managers if they would position the displays near the leading brand?"

"Why not?" Jeff responded. "Based on what Incite Marketing Planning learned, I would ask your representatives to insist on it."

"But that study was conducted in England, not in the United States."

"Mary, people are people. I don't think those who live in England are that different from those who live here."

Mary nodded. "Okay. Now, let's consider the alternative. What if the companies in the United States follow Tesco's lead?"

Jeff turned again to Sarah. "Sarah, why don't you discuss what the team came up with?"

"The team thinks that if Wal-Mart and Kroger follow Tesco's lead, we can do one of two things. One is editing one of the TV spots so it will fit Tesco's in-store TV service. The other is having your company's sales representatives appear in stores in the top 100 markets. Each representative will appear in several stores over five days in a specific market, handing out samples of the chocolate bars."

Mary considered what Sarah presented. "I think the first idea is better than the second."

Jeff asked, "Why's that?"

"I think it would be easier, less expensive, and perhaps more effective for a longer period."

Jeff nodded. "We'll do whatever you request."

"Before you go ahead, let me think about it. If you don't hear from me within three days, call me. Okay?"

After Mary left, Sarah asked Jeff, "What do you think she will do?"

"Knowing Mary, I'd say she will go back to her office, do some research, crunch some numbers, and make a decision soon."

QUESTIONS

1. At the first meeting with Mary, the idea was to use free-standing P-O-P displays in the top 100 markets in the United States. Do you think this is the most suitable form of P-O-P to stimulate sales for a chocolate bar? Why? Why not?

2. Do you think grocers in England and Europe are ahead of those in the United States when it comes to innovation? Explain.

3. Do you think grocers in England and Europe will eliminate free-standing P-O-P displays? Do you think these grocers will restrict advertisers to their in-store TV service? Why? Why not?

4. Sarah mentioned two ideas at the second meeting with Mary. What do you think about these?

5. Can you make other suggestions that will help stimulate sales of the chocolate bar?

6. What problems might prohibit one or more ideas mentioned in the case from being executed? Explain.

West Greenville Convention and Visitors Bureau
How Badly Do You Want a New Account?

EVERY AD AGENCY lives for the opportunity to get a new account. New business invigorates the creative department, gives account people something new to work on, holds the potential for helping the agency financially, and means credit, recognition, and "bragging rights" for the agency. Generally, there are two forms of new business: "all-new" and "organic."

ALL-NEW, NEW BUSINESS

To pitch for "all-new" business, large agencies may spend heavily as they cover the costs of creating a presentation; the costs of materials, travel, and lodgings if necessary; and the work hours invested. Sometimes a new account just "walks in the door." When this happens, the agency's cost to acquire this new account is zero. But this does not happen frequently. It is not uncommon for a large agency going after a large new account to spend in excess of $100,000 on a new business pitch. Even small- to mid-sized agencies can easily spend $30,000–50,000 getting ready for a presentation.

Agency management must balance the amount invested in trying to get an all-new account with the potential revenue expected. Generally, it is difficult to make money on an all-new account in the first year. A rule of thumb is to limit the "external costs" of a new business presentation—the dollars that go "out the door" for such things as research, photography, videos, and materials—to less than 10 percent of the first year's anticipated gross income.

For example, an agency estimates that a potential new client will spend $300,000 in the first year on collateral and print materials. From this total sales figure, you have to subtract the cost-of-sales amount for such things as printing, photography, and other hard costs. What remains will be the agency's commission on the external costs, often 20–25 percent, and the time the art director, copywriters, account people, and others have put into the projects. Let's assume this figure to be $100,000. This is the gross income. Using the 10 percent rule, the agency should not append more than $10,000 on external costs getting ready to pitch for this business.

Agency management has to carefully monitor presentation expenses, because creative people in particular can become so excited about all-new business that they forget to do the math. It would not be prudent to spend much more than $10,000 on outside costs to get a new account that would generate $100,000 of gross income in the first year *unless there are extenuating circumstances*.

Gross income represents the starting point of profitability. The gross income generated by the agency is then used to meet expenses—salaries, rent, utilities, and so forth. What remains after expenses is net income, or net profit—that is, *if* total expenses are less than total gross income. If not, the agency will show a loss.

So, generally, an agency needs to spend prudently to get all-new business and then keep that business for several years in order for it to become a profitable account. What is a profitable account? One where gross income exceeds its share of agency total expenses. How profitable should it be? Generally, agencies will tell you that they want to make a "fair profit" on all work. Sometimes the agency and the client see the definition of "fair" differently.

ORGANIC NEW BUSINESS

Organic new business is additional new business from an existing client. Generally, this business comes to an agency because the agency has performed well on previous client work. If there is no "cost of acquisition," that is, no cost to the agency to get the new business other than answering the phone, this is an ideal situation.

Because the agency staff "knows" the client already, there is virtually no learning curve required. Staff to service the additional business is often in place, and additional staff hiring may not be necessary. Personal relationships are intact, the agency has already proven itself, and organic new business is often absorbed pretty easily.

As an agency helps a client meet opportunities and solve marketing problems, it is often the recipient of organic new business. Do good work; get more of a client's business. This can lead to enhanced profitability for the agency, but it may come at the expense of account diversification. As a client's business grows as a percentage of the agency's total, so too does the danger that if the agency loses that client, the financial impact to the agency could be severe.

When this happens, an agency usually has little choice other than to cut staff. Anyone working on a large account at an ad agency faces this possibility. If the client goes to another ad agency in the same geographic area, the new agency might hire *some* of the key people let go by the first agency. But if the new agency is out of the immediate area, or if the client takes the business "in-house," most likely *all* of those affected by the downsizing will be looking for jobs at other agencies.

NEW BUSINESS CONSIDERATIONS

Since a new large account is one of the fastest ways for an agency to grow, and for the employees to make more money, it might seem that most agencies would jump at the chance to make a presentation, if invited, to get a potentially large, prestigious all-new account. But factors beyond money need to be considered:

- What changes would the agency have to make to service the new account?
- Does the agency have a particular expertise in that line of business?
- Would taking this account preclude the agency from taking another account they would like to have even more?
- Would this account represent a conflict of interest with any account the agency now has?
- Is there anything about the potential client that some agency staff members might not want to be associated with (e.g., a political issue, tobacco products, or alcohol)?
- Would the account be fun to work on?
- Would the account help to advance the position of the agency?
- Can the agency service this account profitably?
- Can the agency afford the investment needed to make the presentation?
- Does the agency have the time to invest in a top-notch presentation?

CONVENTION AND VISITORS BUREAUS

A Convention and Visitors Bureau (CVB) exists to attract visitors and conventions to a particular city. Both groups bring business to a city, not only to the hotels and convention site, but to area businesses as well. Think of the major U.S. cities that attract both groups: Las Vegas, Orlando, New York, and Chicago, for example. What ad agency wouldn't want to be the one that created the multimedia campaign that made these destinations successful? Success by the agency would give it visibility, the accounts seem fun to work on, and a good-sized account like this would probably be a money maker for the agency.

WEST GREENVILLE CONVENTION AND VISITORS BUREAU

A very desirable place to live, West Greenville always had a unique profile. Known as the home of numerous genres of music, West Greenville was made famous by the music that was conceived, written, produced, and recorded within its boundaries. And the West Greenville Convention and Visitors Bureau played an active role in the city's success. In its search for a new ad agency, the West Greenville CVB sent a number of agencies a Request for Proposal (RFP) that asked the usual questions about capability, agency financial standing, size, and how the agency would service its account. From the agencies that responded to the RFP, four were chosen to make presentations.

The ground rules for the presentation drawn up by the West Greenville CVB were:

- Each agency would have 30 minutes to present, and 30 minutes for questions from the CVB board.
- Each agency could present "anything it wanted" to address the needs of West Greenville to attract vacation visitors and conventions.
- Each agency would be given $2,500 to offset the cost of the presentation. All creative materials and business-building ideas presented would become the property of the CVB once the agency cashed the check.
- Each agency was to propose a budget to get the job done. It was generally thought that West Greenville would spend "about" $100,000 a year to promote visitation.

QUESTIONS

1. If you were part of the management of one of the four agencies going to pitch for the West Greenville CVB account, what would you be thinking?
2. What are the considerations and ramifications of pitching?
3. If you were CEO of one of the four agencies, what would your pitch strategy be?
4. Should your agency present in light of the CVB's ground rules?
5. What risks and rewards do you see for the agency?

Chantillon Champagne

CALIFORNIA VINTNERS, INC., a major producer of domestic wines, is located in Modesto, California. The company has a long history of successfully producing and distributing a complete line of table wines under its Scolari label. The company was founded in 1954 by Antonio Scolari, a 28-year-old immigrant. Scolari learned the vintner's art from his father, who practiced it throughout his lifetime in Italy. Antonio saw no future for himself in Italy and decided to emigrate to the United States, which offered greater promise of success.

Antonio arrived in New York in 1953 with little money. His meager possessions included several different varieties of grape vines that he pruned from his father's vineyards. Antonio lived with relatives and friends in New York until he was able to accumulate sufficient funds to move to California. He settled in Modesto because its climate closely approximated that of his native Italy. Antonio invested the remainder of his money in land that he believed could be cultivated as vineyards. He planted the vine strands and began to till the land. From his modest annual grape harvest, he produced wines that he sold to dealers in Modesto.

By continually reinvesting his profits over a 30-year period, Antonio accumulated thousands of acres of new vineyards as well as the most modern wine-producing equipment available. His operation grew steadily during this period, and his winery became the eighth largest in California, with annual sales of $80 million. In 1985 Antonio suffered a severe heart attack. Since he had never married, he had no heirs. As his health gradually deteriorated, he was forced to sell the winery to a group of California investors, who incorporated under the title of California Vintners, Inc. (CVI).

This case was prepared by Joseph R. Pisani, Ph.D., professor emeritus, Department of Advertising, College of Journalism and Communications, University of Florida, Gainesville.

With a fresh injection of capital and new management, the company expanded its operations over the next 10 years. In 1995 annual sales reached $150 million, and CVI became the fifth largest California winery.

In 1999 top management decided to produce and market domestic champagne. CVI had experimented with champagne over a 10-year period. They knew that the European process produced superior champagne. The major disadvantage in using this approach, however, was its high cost. An alternative process had been developed by a competing California winery, which halved the cost of the European process and required a far shorter aging period. Its major drawback was that it resulted in some loss of product quality. The process was licensed to other American producers, who quickly began to mass produce champagne.

CVI decided to enter into a licensing agreement to obtain the rights to the American process. The company's marketing objective was to expand the market for domestic champagne by aiming for a mass market rather than "connoisseurs." There were several reasons for adopting this approach:

(1) Since the American process was less costly, the champagne could sell for a price one-half to two-thirds lower than the price of imported champagne. The price would be within the reach of middle-income households, which the company viewed as its primary market.

(2) A lower price would encourage greater use, since families might not limit their consumption of champagne to special occasions.

(3) The company did not consider the American process's loss of quality a serious drawback because it would be compensated for by the lower price. The loss in quality would most likely be noticeable only to champagne connoisseurs, who were not the primary target market. The true connoisseur would purchase an imported brand anyway, because of its superior quality. A significant change in the attitudes of the connoisseur market would require a product superior or, at the very least, comparable in quality to European champagnes, as well as considerable advertising and promotion expenditures to overcome their objections to a domestically produced quality champagne.

(4) CVI's champagne was superior to other domestically produced champagnes because of a longer and more careful aging process. This special process had been developed by the company and represented a genuine improvement over the licensed American process. When used in conjunction with the American process, the unique aging process resulted in a superior product. The special aging process required a period of eight years and added to the costs of using the American process. But the company believed that the sales volume resulting from a wider market would cover the added cost and yield a minimum return of 10 percent of sales.

(5) The connoisseur market segment was simply too small. It did not offer the unlimited sales potential of the much larger middle-income market.

(6) Other American producers had aimed their marketing effort at the connoisseur market with little tangible success. No American producer previously had attempted to reach the middle-income market.

Tom Anderson, CVI's vice president of marketing, was directed by top management to begin test marketing the champagne in February 2000. Since approximately 40 percent of U.S. wine and champagne is consumed in California annually, Anderson established the test market in a medium-sized California city that contained a high proportion of middle-income families. Approximately 50 percent of these families were classified as heavy users of wine. About 15 percent of the heavy users consumed Scolari wines.

The test market results were promising. Research indicated that the heavy wine users had a favorable attitude toward champagne. In blind taste tests against competing domestically produced champagnes, the CVI brand was most preferred. Approximately 70 percent of the test participants rated the CVI champagne superior to the other brands.

Several proposed brand names were tested. The name *Chantillon* appeared to have the highest consumer acceptance. Research also indicated that the more distinctive the brand's name, the higher the champagne's sales potential. Anderson adopted the name *Chantillon* because test participants found it to be distinctive and also felt that it gave the wine a "French" or "imported" flavor. The choice of *Chantillon* was a departure from tradition, because champagnes normally use the winery name as the brand name. But the name *Scolari* had been rejected by test participants as a proposed name for the champagne because it sounded too "Italian." The test market disclosed several other important factors:

(1) Middle-income families in the test market attached a price–quality relationship to their purchase of champagne. This view is essentially correct because champagnes are priced according to their quality. Vintage champagnes are priced much higher than nonvintage champagnes by both the domestic and foreign industries. Vintages refer to the quality of the grape harvest used in producing champagne for the year. If the grape harvest is of exceptional quality, the champagne is given a vintage rating and commands a higher selling price. Grape harvests of poorer quality result in a nonvintage rating because the champagne is blended with remaining quantities of champagne from good or exceptional years and thereby commands a lower price. The quality of the grape harvest depends primarily on weather and growing conditions. The fertility of the soil is not as critical, because grapes will prosper in poor soil in most temperate climates. The age of the champagne is also a factor. As it grows older, its price will rise. This is particularly true of vintage champagnes that are ready for drinking after six years of aging and can reach an age of approximately 12 years with no loss in quality.

(2) Middle-income families in the test market viewed champagne as a drink to be consumed only on special occasions. However, 60 percent of the families interviewed indicated that they would purchase and drink champagne more often if prices were lower.

(3) Approximately 20 percent of the families interviewed stated that they purchased champagne on impulse and often relied on the recommendation of the retailer.

THE CASE

Armed with the results of the test market, Tom Anderson persuaded top management to introduce Chantillon in California. If the first year's sales results were promising, a decision would be made the following year on whether to market Chantillon nationally. A $3.5 million integrated marketing communications budget was allocated to introduce the product. All promotions would be planned and executed by the company's advertising department. The company's sales force would be assigned the job of persuading wholesalers and retailers to distribute the product. Distribution was not viewed as a major problem because CVI already had a well-established distribution system for its Scolari line.

Chantillon was priced at approximately one-half the price of imported champagnes and approximately 20 percent higher than competing domestic champagnes. Anderson's reasoning was based on two factors: (1) Chantillon could not compete directly with imported champagnes because it was not of comparable quality; and (2) Chantillon was superior in quality to domestic champagnes and more costly to produce, which justified its higher price. The price differential would also serve to enhance Chantillon's quality image over competing domestic brands of champagne. Both of these factors were supported by the test market results.

The advertising creative strategy was centered on the general theme of offering a quality champagne at an affordable price. The new campaign was built around the unifying theme "The Quiet One." The copy explained that, contrary to popular belief, quality champagnes do not make a loud popping noise when opened. Chantillon was called "The Quiet One" because it opened more quietly, an attribute that provided evidence of its superior quality. The copy stressed that the special aging process was responsible for Chantillon's quality and slightly higher price.

The expenditures for the Chantillon Champagne media plan are shown in table 35.1. Approximately one-half of the cable television budget was to be spent during the first two months of the campaign. Cable TV was selected as the primary medium because of its high potential coverage of a specific target market at a low cost relative to network television. Cable's ability to create awareness and impact is essential when introducing a new product. The expenditures in other media reinforce the impact and awareness created by television. The balance of the plan called for the spacing of expenditures over the remaining 10 months in order to attain the desired levels of reach, frequency, and continuity. Media were selected based on their ability to deliver the specific target audience. Anderson believed that the company must sacrifice some wasted coverage in most of these supporting media choices in order to gain maximum awareness and impact among true prospects in the viewing audience.

The media plan allocated $550,000 for newspaper cooperative advertising with participating retailers. The cooperative funds were to be allocated on proportionally equal terms to retailers in the form of advertising allowances. The purpose of these allowances

TABLE 35.1
Chantillon Champagne Media Plan Expenditures

Cable television	$1,300,000
Radio	100,000
Mass circulation magazines (western regional editions)	400,000
Newspapers (cooperative advertising)	550,000
Sunday supplements	100,000
Special-interest magazines	200,000
Transit advertising	100,000
Outdoor advertising	250,000
Internet advertising (search engines and wine retailer sites)	100,000
Point-of-purchase displays	400,000
Total	$3,500,000

was to encourage retailers to recommend Chantillon to customers who inquired about champagne. An additional $400,000 was allocated for in-store displays and promotions. Anderson based these allocations on the research finding that a portion of the test market purchased champagne on impulse.

Chantillon sales during its first year on the market reached $15 million. CVI realized a return on sales of 3 percent. The marketing goal for the first year was at best to break even. Needless to say, Anderson was highly encouraged by the promising numbers.

During the year, the primary demand for domestic champagne increased by 10 percent, largely due to CVI's introductory marketing effort. Chantillon attained a 15 percent share of this larger market. CVI's management also was pleased with Chantillon's performance and decided to gradually enter into national distribution during the coming year. Anderson realized that national distribution would require a greater volume of advertising and promotion expenditures than what was appropriated for the California market.

The company's advertising department was not large enough in terms of personnel and facilities to handle the necessary advertising volume. Anderson also believed that a fresh creative approach would be needed during the coming year, despite the success of the preceding year's campaign. For these reasons, Anderson recommended that CVI retain an advertising agency for the Chantillon account. Top management agreed, and Anderson prepared a list of advertising agencies that might be suitable for servicing the account. Top management reviewed the list and selected five agencies, each of whom was invited to make a presentation for the account.

One of the lucky five was the Bailey Limon Group, a medium-sized, full-service agency based in New York City. Sheila Bailey, the head of Bailey Limon, started concentrating on the presentation her agency would make to the CVI executives for the Chantillon account.

QUESTIONS

1. What criteria would you suggest that the CVI top management consider in making their selection of an advertising agency for the Chantillon account?
2. If you were Sheila Bailey, what system of compensation for your agency would you suggest to the executives of CVI? Give reasons supporting your choice.
3. Assume that the Bailey Limon Group has determined CVI's research to be inadequate and that in their presentation they will propose further research. Draw up a recommended research proposal that includes answers to the following questions:
   a. What type of research would you recommend be undertaken?
   b. What factors about the product and the market would you want your research to uncover?
   c. What economic and demographic characteristics of consumers of champagne would you consider to be salient to your research?
   d. What factors regarding consumer behavior would you expect your research to uncover?
   e. Outline the major steps that you would take in performing your research and give a summary of your research plan.
4. Using your anticipated research conclusions as a basis, what creative strategy should Bailey Limon recommend to CVI for the forthcoming national advertising campaign for Chantillon?
5. What advertising appropriation should Bailey Limon recommend for implementing the advertising strategy? What method should they use to determine the size of their appropriation?
6. What media strategy should Bailey Limon recommend for Chantillon? How should they allocate their appropriation among the various media?

PizzaTown, Inc.
Media Planning and Budgeting

AFTER WORKING several really late evenings over the past week at the Stirling agency, Debbie Post was feeling pleased that the budget she would present tomorrow to Rick Blacksburg, her supervisor, was finally taking shape. After all, doing the media planning to recommend how to invest more than $25 million in media was not a task to be taken lightly. Rick had warned Debbie that Randy Robinson, vice president of media services for Stirling's client PizzaTown, was a tough and savvy "media expert" who held some very specific ideas as to what his company's media plan should look like. Once Debbie and Rick were comfortable with their agency's media recommendations, they would arrange an appointment to present them to Randy Robinson.

PizzaTown had recently created the VP of media services position to help answer the questions that company senior management always asked when reviewing the media recommendations prepared by the ad agency:

Are we getting the most efficient and effective media plan we can for our $25 million?
Are we spending our money on the right media classes?
Are we targeting our media to the most effective geographical locations?
Are we using too much TV?

These questions, and many more, were sure to come up when the agency presented its recommendations to Randy Robinson at PizzaTown.

BACKGROUND

PizzaTown—or PT, as it is called by most of its customers—is a chain of quick-service restaurants (QSRs) that offer both dine-in service as well as home delivery, with prices slightly higher than those of its competitors. There are more than 300 PT restaurants in the continental United States. Many are located in the crowded Northeast, while most of the chain's expansion is occurring in the Sunbelt states.

Research has shown that many of the customers are male, 18–35 years of age, high school graduates, holding jobs in construction, distribution, or retailing. Because the newest restaurants feature outdoor patios, a Friday- or Saturday-night family visit to PT has become very popular, particularly in the Southeast. Generally, young families can enjoy a PT "Monster" pizza with drinks and salad for around $20. Also available is the popular buffet line, with "all the pizza you care to eat" for just $5.99, plus drink and tax.

As a food, pizza saw enormous growth in the 1970s and 1980s. But lately a trend has been developing for more "authentic" ethnic foods, such as Asian, Indian, and Mexican.

Debbie and Rick at the Stirling agency, and Randy Robinson at PizzaTown, knew that it was getting more and more expensive to "reach" their desired audiences. Past media plans always recommended plenty of TV, because with its wide audience reach and ability to offer compelling visual images, it was thought to be the perfect medium. With the cost of TV media constantly rising, and audiences shrinking, and every other restaurant chain using TV, was there a better way for PT to reach its target audiences?

RANDY ROBINSON

After spending the past six years at one of the best-known media buying agencies in the United States, and before that more than 15 years at a major New York ad agency, Roscoe "Randy" Robinson decided to accept PizzaTown's offer to become its first "in-house" media expert. The position was created after PT's senior vice president of operations had attended a seminar on "Ad Agency Accountability," sponsored by the American Association of Advertising Agencies (AAAA). It wasn't that the operations VP felt the Stirling agency was doing anything wrong; it's just that he wanted to feel more comfortable that PT had someone "in-house" who could better assess the agency's media plans and recommendations. PizzaTown needed someone who could review the effectiveness and wisdom of the myriad media choices Stirling would have regarding where to place PT's messages.

The upcoming meeting with Debbie and Rick would be Randy's first meeting with the Stirling agency since joining PT five months ago.

PIZZATOWN STORE MANAGERS

In many ways, PT's store managers and assistant managers are typical of others in the restaurant industry. All know that to be successful, a manager has to show stable if not growing sales, and the restaurant has to score well in inspections by the Health

Department. It is also the manager's responsibility to see that the restaurant staff are courteous, friendly, and well trained.

To maintain and grow sales, each manager relies on promotions and point-of-sale material from PT's main office, as well as media advertising targeted directly at the primary audiences that would find a visit to a PizzaTown an enjoyable experience. For the past three years, PizzaTown has asked selected managers to participate with the corporate marketing department to evaluate its advertising. Each year, management has heard basically the same feedback:

"We don't need pretty advertising, we need hard hitting stuff."

"The ads need to highlight deals and specials."

"We need something to overcome our more expensive prices."

"We need more families, especially during the week."

"Advertise price specials with more frequency, in more places, LOUDLY."

"Subtle messages don't fill my restaurant."

DEBBIE POST'S CHECKLIST

As the media plan that Debbie would present to Rick was printing, Debbie reached across her desk to retrieve a crumpled sheet of yellow legal-pad paper. She thought she would make one final check of the lists that she had jotted down almost two weeks ago, when she first began to create her plan on what to recommend to PizzaTown regarding the $25 million they were budgeting for media. Had she covered all the bases? Had she carefully considered the alternatives? Was her research current enough about the competition, media costs, audience delivery figures, and the changing role of TV? Smoothing out the wrinkled yellow sheet, Debbie reviewed her rough chart, depicted in table 36.1.

Her plan was to recommend that PT spend almost 65 percent of its budget using TV, mostly in the Northeast because of the high concentration of stores. Other than TV, the next largest chunks of PT's budget would go to outdoor advertising and local newspapers, where coupon ads and special deals on a market-by-market basis could appear. She was uncertain about the impact of radio, and she knew the agency had not recommended it much in the past. But she had heard from a friend of hers who worked for a large radio station that Randy Robinson *loved* radio and would probably want to see it on any recommendation made by the agency.

Then a cold wave of panic elevated her heartbeat. Her palms were clammy. *"I LOVE this job!"* Debbie thought. Then she focused. "Rick wants to look good with Randy Robinson. Have I pushed this plan far enough? With what my instinct tells me about TV, at least the way I watch it, maybe it's losing its effectiveness. Should I revise the media plan to include radio?"

And finally, "Will I look like a *trainee*, or worse *an intern*, when Randy Robinson sees this plan? Good thing Rick is going over it tomorrow. Can I defend my budget decisions?"

TABLE 36.1

Media Plan for the PizzaTown Account

TV/Newspapers
Network?
Cable?
Sports? What day?
Sunday?
How big are the ads?
Use "alternative" papers?
What section of the paper? *Scheduling*
Weekdays?
Evenings?
Prime Time?
A few ads on popular programs?
Lots of ads on lots of programs?
Established markets or new markets? *Measurement*
Effectiveness[a]
Efficiency[b]

[a]Effectiveness = the degree to which the target audience is reached
[b]Efficiency = Effectiveness ÷ Media cost

QUESTIONS

1. What should Debbie say to Rick tomorrow? Why?
2. Is TV dead as a means to reach today's fractured audiences? Provide support for your answer.
3. Should Debbie's media plan be revised to include radio? Give arguments for and against doing this.
4. Do you agree with the decision to advertise primarily in the Northeast? Why, or why not?
5. What do you think about "warm and fuzzy" ads versus loud ads that shout "2 Pizzas for $11!"?
6. What makes sense to you regarding where Debbie should have started her planning? Why?
7. Should the ad agency, or the advertising itself, be held accountable for PT's sales? Explain your reasoning.

The Design Circus
Employees Having an Affair

THE DESIGN CIRCUS (TDC), a small 12-person design studio and ad agency, is located in a mid-sized town in rural South Carolina. Founded six years ago to serve a small bank holding company headquartered in the same town, TDC has grown slowly but steadily and now employs a staff of six designers, an editor, two mechanical artists, an illustrator, and a media buyer. The twelfth person is the company founder, Mike Fox, an entrepreneur with a background in sales and marketing. Three people report to Mike: the editor, the media buyer, and Dan, who supervises the six designers, two mechanical artists, and the illustrator.

In most small design companies, employees are called upon to perform multiple "nondesigner" tasks, and often those duties fall outside any job description that might exist. Among the things that might need to be done on a daily basis are ordering supplies, keeping the soft-drink machine stocked, running the dishwasher, keeping the kitchen clean, and emptying the recycling bin.

At the same time, all designers are expected to record on daily time sheets their billing for as many as six hours each day, just as many law firms do. This selling of "time," and the marking up of outside purchases made on behalf of the client's name, are the way most agencies and design firms make money today.

On most days, everyone is busy all of the time. The culture at TDC could best be described as collaborative and congenial, but also fast-paced and a bit "out there." Some years ago, TDC created an employee manual as protection against certain behaviors. For example, it was explicitly stated that firearms were prohibited on the premises, that any employee whose work suffered because of substance abuse on or off the job would be immediately terminated, and that sexual harassment in any form would not be tolerated.

It is not difficult to understand why an employer would ban firearms, or not look favorably on an employee whose job performance was compromised by substance abuse. Likewise, most managers are aware of lawsuits brought against other employers, big and small, from an employee charging sexual harassment. Most of the time the charges come from a female employee and are brought against a male co-worker or the company. But the reverse happens, as does same-sex harassment.

SEXUAL HARASSMENT

Sexual harassment is a legal concept developed originally to address a particular type of sexual discrimination. Briefly, sexual harassment is unwelcome behavior of a sexual nature that makes someone feel uncomfortable or unwelcome in the workplace by focusing attention on one's gender instead of on one's professional qualifications. The concept applies now to both women and men, to adults and to children.

Sexual harassment is usually defined as behavior by someone higher in status or power toward someone lower in status or power, although harassment by peers or customers is also recognized as a problem. The unequal balance of power is an intrinsic element of the legal definition of sexual harassment.

Sexual harassment is conduct characterized by repeated and undesired words, acts, or gestures with a sexual connotation which by nature attack the dignity or the physical or psychological integrity of a person or lead to unfavorable working and learning conditions or dismissal. Sexual harassment corresponds to those behaviors with a sexual connotation that are unilateral and undesired and that attack a person's well-being and human rights.

Such behavior may take a variety of forms including but not limited to:

- Persistent manifestations of sexual interest on the part of someone who knows or can reasonably know that such interest is not wished.
- Verbal advances already refused and nevertheless repeated without the consent of the person who is the object of those advances.
- Insistent and undesired propositions of a sexual nature.
- Systematic or incessant sexual remarks or comments made in front of several persons when this is done to intimidate others in that group.
- Nonconsensual physical advances such as touching, caressing, brushing against, pinching, or kissing.
- Remarks, comments, allusions, jokes, or insults of a sexual nature that are repeated or continual and that disturb the atmosphere of work or study.
- An explicit or implicit promise of reward or favorable treatment in return for complying with requests of a sexual nature.
- An implicit or explicit threat of retribution or unfavorable, hostile, unjust, or discriminatory treatment if a person refuses to submit to a request of a sexual nature, or the reprisals that effectively follow such a refusal.

- Voyeurism or exhibitionism.
- Attitudes or acts of physical aggression or assault with the intention of imposing an undesired sexual intimacy.
- Persistent, unwanted contact or attention after the end of a consensual relationship.
- Sexually degrading language used to describe a person.
- All other offensive manifestations of a sexual nature.

THE CASE

Dan, a close personal friend of Mike, is a very talented art director and was recruited to join TDC when Mike founded the company. Dan's drive, his 24/7 "get-it-done" attitude, and his creative talent have played a huge role in the success of TDC. In his late 30s, Dan lives in the fast lane. He loves fast cars, motorcycles, and working out. He is smart, aggressive, and confident of his abilities. Only after Dan has thoroughly interviewed a candidate will TDC hire the person as one of its many talented young designers. It is this group, and the work they do for TDC's clients, that makes the little design firm so successful.

Jenny is one of TDC's newest employees. She, her husband, and their five-year-old son were brought to town about a year ago by TDC. This move was necessitated by TDC's win of the large Stratus Cellular account, an account that required media planning and placement. Since TDC is the only creative services firm of any size in the town where it is located, Jenny had to be recruited from another market, since TDC was unable to find a qualified media planner in its own town.

At most agencies, media people and creative people are encouraged to work together on creative materials that will appear in the media. The media planner may have to create a media plan based on predetermined ad sizes. The ad sizes that are used will be a function of the client's budget, the media where the ads run, the need for creative impact, and the communication message. It makes little sense for the media planner to do a media plan and budget for half-page, black-and-white ads when the creative people are thinking full-page, four-color ads. All of these decisions—creative and media—are based on the overall marketing strategy, the creative strategy, and the media strategy.

At first, no one thought much about the amount of time Dan and Jenny were spending together. Since they were working on the agency's biggest client, this was expected. Over time, some began to notice telltale signs of an office romance. On days Dan called in sick, so did Jenny. The timesheets of both employees showed that they were both working long hours, often on the same days. Employees sometimes found themselves answering calls from Jenny's husband, who thought she was working late. Dan's phone was often busy, but not from outside calls. One thing no one missed was the nonverbal communication between Dan and Jenny when they were together in a meeting.

Finally Mike notices their behavior and doesn't know what to do, or if he should do anything. He has heard rumors that Jenny's husband has a problem with alcohol, but he hasn't observed anything to make these rumors seem believable. Besides, what Jenny's husband does is none of Mike's business. Mike's concern is that Dan and Jenny, both important to the agency's largest account, could be having an affair both on and off company time. But there is no proof that anything they are doing is inappropriate or harmful to the agency.

Lots of facts and thoughts have been spinning in Mike's head. Dan isn't married; Jenny is. Dan could be replaced on the Stratus Cellular business more easily than could Jenny. Dan and Mike have been friends for 10 years. Is someone coercing someone, or is the affair consensual? Does that make any difference? Dan is senior to Jenny, but Jenny doesn't work directly for Dan. Is their affair in any way affecting the agency? Could it become an issue with Stratus Cellular if Mike has to fire one or both of them? What are the legal ramifications? Could Jenny's husband sue Mike or the agency for not putting a stop to what is happening?

If Mike does nothing, maybe the affair would just burn out and things would return to normal. This could happen. But what if the affair ended badly for Jenny and she sued TDC for sexual harassment, saying that Dan used his position of authority to pressure her into the relationship, or that TDC condoned a "hostile workplace"? And suppose the relationship ended badly for Dan. Might he threaten to quit if Jenny wasn't fired? Suppose neither quit. What might this mean for TDC and Stratus Cingular? And what about Jenny's husband? Could he become violent?

QUESTIONS

1. What should Mike do, if anything? Should he fire anyone? Should he just wait?
2. Suppose there is a consensual affair taking place. Is it any of Mike's business?
3. Should Mike say anything to the rest of the staff?
4. What should Mike do if Jenny's husband calls to confront him with his suspicions?
5. Should companies make it a policy that co-workers who have affairs will be fired? Why, or why not?

Maria's Code of Ethics

MARIA LOPEZ worked several years as an account executive in an advertising agency before she pursued a graduate degree in marketing at one of the top business schools in Tennessee. After her graduation, she accepted a job at Keller Advertising, an agency in Memphis. She thought that as an account executive at Keller, she would have an opportunity to apply what she had learned in business school.

Now Maria was standing with her boss Rick Johnson and several others from the Keller agency near the bar that had been set up in the hotel where the Addy Awards was being held. They were talking about sports when Jim Keller, the president of the agency, arrived and joined them.

"Hello, people," he said. "How are you?"

"Fine, Jim," several said, almost in unison. "And you?"

"Fine, thank you." He laughed. Then he noticed that Maria's drink was almost empty. "Do you need another?"

"No, I'm okay," she said.

Then a voice coming from speakers positioned throughout the room told them, "Please take your seats at your tables. Our dinners are being served. We will announce the winners after the last person has been served. If you hear your name, please come to the stage to receive your award."

Jim, Maria, Rick, and the others from the agency soon found their tables and sat down. Maria and Erin Walters, who worked in creative, were seated together and had a lively conversation while they ate their dinners. Maria noticed that every time the agency won an award, Jim Keller's name was announced as the winner or co-winner. She nudged Erin after the fifth time she heard Jim's name, and Erin provided an explanation. Maria knew she would have to talk to Rick at some point about what she had just heard.

Later, everyone from the agency returned to the bar, where Jim announced that he was buying the next two rounds of drinks. After the third drink, Maria was feeling lightheaded.

Jim approached her. "Do you need another, Maria?"

She laughed and replied, "No, I'm okay. How about you? Are you okay?"

Jim laughed and glanced at Rick Johnson. Rick noticed Jim's glance and walked over. "Well, Jim, we had a great night," Rick said. "I think we walked away with 46 awards."

Jim nodded. "Yes, we should be proud of the work we've done for our clients."

Maria suddenly excused herself and went to the restroom. When she returned, Jim and Rick looked at her.

Rick asked, "Are you okay?" Maria nodded, but she didn't feel okay.

"I think someone should drive you home," Jim said.

"I'm fine, Jim," she said.

"Are you sure?"

Maria didn't answer. She turned and walked quickly to the restroom. When she returned, she found Rick and asked, "Rick, would you mind driving me home? I'm not feeling well."

"No problem. Jim will follow in his car and bring me back."

Maria missed work the next day; she called in sick. The following day, however, as soon as she arrived, Rick entered her office and sat down.

"Are you okay, Maria?"

"Yes. Thanks for driving me home."

"I was happy to do it." Then Rick changed the subject. "Maria, do you remember seeing the ads for Carmichael Industries?"

Maria nodded and replied, "Yes, why?"

"Well, someone had the audacity to remove Jim's name from them. Jim had a call this morning from Ed Carmichael and found out his name wasn't on the ads."

"I know. I removed Jim's name before I gave the ads to Larry."

"Why did you remove Jim's name?"

"Because he was not the creative director on that job."

"Maria, I know that and you know that, but around here Jim's name goes on every piece of work, no matter who does the work."

"I don't understand that, Rick."

"Maria, he's the president of the agency."

"I know that."

"Jim claims that every client we have expects to see his name on their ads, no matter whether he's involved or not."

Maria shook her head. "I find that hard to believe, considering the size of this agency. In fact, it's one of the largest agencies in Memphis."

"You've been talking to Erin Walters, haven't you?"

Maria looked confused. "What do you mean?"

"I saw you two at the awards banquet. I bet she told you that she's been the creative director on a number of projects, didn't she?"

Maria nodded.

"I bet she told you that she never got the credit she deserves. Am I right?"

Maria sighed. "She said that Jim insists on having his name on every project, even when he isn't involved in the project. She told me that he's taken credit on projects that she's done."

Rick nodded and said, "That's true."

"Well, that's not right."

Rick leaned forward in his chair. "I know it's not right, but that's how things are done here. And I know that's how things are done at some other agencies."

"Erin told me that she started working here right after Jim opened the agency. That was a long time ago. She said that he served as the creative director on every project in those days."

"That's true," Rick said.

"She said that as the agency grew, Jim had to devote his time to managing the agency, not serving as the agency's creative director."

"I know," Rick said.

"She also said that when the creative staff works overtime, they are paid the regular hourly rate, not time and a half."

Rick nodded. "That's true."

"Well, I don't think that's right. I think you need to meet with the creative directors, including Erin, and ask them how they feel about Jim putting his name on their hard work. Then I think you need to meet with every member of the creative staff and ask them how they feel about being paid the same hourly rate when they work overtime. I think they will be in favor of being paid time and a half."

Rick leaned back and closed his eyes for a few moments. When he opened them, he said, "Maria, I think I know how the creative directors feel, but Jim is the president."

"Rick, this is a big agency now. There are several creative directors, not one or two. It isn't fair to them."

"Jim is the founder and the president. He can put his name on everything. That's the way it is."

Maria shook her head. "I disagree, and I think you need to meet with the creative directors. Ask them how they feel about Jim receiving credit as the creative director when he shouldn't."

Rick looked at her quietly for a moment and then said, "Let's say that I have a meeting and the creative directors think that Jim's name should not appear on their respective projects. What then?"

"Then you inform Jim."

"That's easy for you to say," Rick said.

"Then I'll inform him."

Rick smiled and said, "I bet you would." He stood up and walked to the door.

"Rick, you know it's not ethical for him to receive credit for others' hard work. And you also know it's not ethical for him not to pay employees time and a half when they deserve it for overtime."

Rick nodded and left.

QUESTIONS

1. Does Maria have a legitimate complaint about Jim receiving credit for other people's work? Why, or why not?
2. Do you think Rick will meet with the creative directors? If he does meet with them, what do you think he should say or ask? What would you do if you were in his position? Would you have a meeting?
3. Do you think Maria is out of line by asking Rick, her supervisor, to have a meeting with the creative directors? Why, or why not?
4. Do you think Maria's code of ethics is similar to yours? Do you think her heart is in the right place? Explain.
5. Do you think Maria may get into trouble if Jim learns about her suggestion? Why? Why not?
6. Are there other potential problems for Maria or Rick? Are there potential problems for Erin?
7. Is Maria's complaint about the employees not being paid time and a half for overtime justified? Why, or why not?
8. Do you think Rick will meet with every member of the creative staff about overtime pay? Why, or why not? If you were in Rick's position, what would you do?

The Museum Board of the State of California
What If You Don't Like the Creative Product?

ANGELA GRAHAM, an up and coming account executive at NorthSouth Advertising, left the Museum Board offices with her mind racing. She tried to sort out the implications of the meeting she had just attended. While there were many issues to address, one thing seemed clear. Once she got back to the agency, and the news spread, it would become the kind of afternoon she hated. In the high-pressure and elevated-ego world of advertising, Angela knew that personal confrontations and professional questioning were always just around the corner.

The Museum Board of the State of California was Angela's largest client. NorthSouth had been working feverishly for several weeks to produce layouts and recommendations for a new campaign, including both magazine advertising and broadcast creative, to support the Museum Board's newest museum just outside San Diego. Angela was excited about the new account and the assignment. The new museum had been open for only two months, and she knew that NorthSouth's creative materials were important for bringing students and teachers to the museum.

The purpose of the new museum was to chronicle and showcase the history of public education in California. Named "Classes through Time," the museum was a state-of-the-art display and interactive experience that schoolchildren seemed to like. Group visitation was slowly building, mainly by word-of-mouth recommendations among teachers. NorthSouth had been hired to spread the word more effectively and increase visitation to an annual rate of 50,000 students from all over the state. Over the first two months, about 400 students and their teachers had visited, mostly from around the San Diego area. Teachers who had visited were outspoken in their praise.

For more than a week prior to her presentation of the new campaign, however, Angela had been sick with the flu that had struck about a quarter of the NorthSouth staff. The usual back and forth between the Creative and Account Service departments over the materials, therefore, took place without Angela. The first time she saw the layouts for the print ads and the storyboards for TV was the morning before she was to present the campaign. Her initial uneasiness about what the creative staff had in mind for the campaign now turned into dismay. The creative direction seemed all wrong. And what's more, she thought it was embarrassing and demeaning to the audience it was intended to register with.

Angela's first action was to talk to her supervisor, Tom Huang. Tom, several years more experienced than Angela, listened thoughtfully, said he somewhat agreed, but concluded, "It isn't worth starting World War III over." Tom suggested that maybe Angela was overreacting, and he reminded her that, by being sick, she missed several important strategic meetings where the creative was discussed. "That would have been the time to express any reservations," Tom said, "and now it's way too late."

Tom also reminded her that the moving force behind the campaign and the creative executions was Stephen Miles, a young but upwardly mobile art director known for his "edgy" work. Stephen was forever telling anyone who would listen that "work must be controversial to get noticed" and that "vanilla tastes bad." Both statements reflected his very strong opinions about creative work and advertising.

Angela thought she understood where Stephen and his work for the Museum Board were coming from. She had repeatedly heard him brag about awards he had won at a previous agency.

"He doesn't give a damn about the Classes through Time Museum or its intended audience," Angela said to Tom. "He's just looking to build his own reputation!" The more she thought about it, the madder she got. "The ads might appeal to Stephen or other edgy art directors, but not teachers!"

Tom just shrugged and headed for the coffee machine, leaving Angela to her uneasy premonitions about the next day's meeting with the client. "Stephen's just trying to prove he can steamroll a stodgy Museum Board," she thought. "He thinks this is all about him, and how clever he is!"

With neither time on her side nor allies to support her criticism that the creative was off-target and somewhat offensive, Angela realized she had to prepare for her meeting. But, she wondered, "How can I present and sell work I don't like or agree with? Should I tell the board I don't agree with the direction represented? What if the board, by virtue of its lack of experience or timidity, accepts the campaign? What if the campaign then fails or embarrasses the board? Could the agency be fired?"

At the meeting, Angela knew almost immediately that her worst fears had been realized. As she made the presentation, some of the Museum Board members offered little or no comment, but several who were former educators objected vehemently to the ads and TV commercials that were being proposed. Using words like "demeaning," "potty-humor," "embarrassing," and "amateurish," they ripped apart the creative executions that showed educators in uncomfortable, compromising, and stereotypical classroom situations. Male teachers were represented as wearing outlandish ties, and female teachers all looked like prim and proper matrons. Throughout the ads and TV commercials were spitballs, badly behaving children, annoying parents, poor cafeteria food, dumb administrators, and classroom "personal accidents."

The tagline on the ads was, "A day at the Museum has to be better than THIS!" The copy suggested that a trip to the museum would replace a dysfunctional classroom with a place to learn.

During the presentation, Angela felt humiliated, compromised, and unprofessional. As she drove back to the NorthSouth offices, she thought about her arrival there and the report she would have to make.

QUESTIONS

1. What should Angela do when she gets back to the agency? Should she go directly to Stephen Miles and tell him what the Museum Board members said?
2. Should Angela have told Stephen she had reservations about the campaign before it was presented? Should Angela have started World War III? With whom would she have started it?
3. Discuss the notion of "what I don't like" versus "what will work."
4. Who is responsible at the agency for the museum's success?
5. Are awards really that important? Why do creative people want them? What role do awards play in advertising and marketing?
6. Where or when should good taste come into play in advertising?
7. Do ads have to be controversial to get noticed or to work? Explain.
8. How does the audience figure into what should be presented?
9. What is "edgy" creative execution? Do you think it can be necessary? Does edgy always have to equate to "tasteless"? Do you think it is an effective technique? Give some examples from advertising you have seen.

Pete Boswell, Account Executive
Dealing with a Bad Boss

PETE BOSWELL was one of the lucky students in his graduating class at State University. Despite a sluggish hiring environment among advertising agencies across the Southeast, Pete received job offers from two highly respected and successful ad agencies. After much deliberation and discussions with his faculty advisor at State University, Pete accepted the offer made by Brunner Advertising. What made this decision even tougher was that the other agency had made an eleventh-hour counter-offer that added $5,000 to their initial offer plus a signing bonus of $3,000! But Pete, one of the highest achieving and brightest students to ever go through the advertising program at State University, made his decision based on his careful evaluation of Brunner's culture, his chances for rapid advancement, the clients he would be working with, and the people he had met. He was very careful to thank the second agency for its generous offer; he didn't want to burn any bridges in case the Brunner position didn't work out.

The first few weeks at Brunner were as exciting as he had imagined. The agency had a cool building, some great clients, and a work ethic that matched Pete's "can do" spirit. With his orientation just about complete, Pete knew he had made the right decision to join Brunner Advertising.

After the orientation period, Pete was to report to Carol Lipscomb, an account supervisor with a great reputation for training and developing newcomers. Carol was seen as a rising star at Brunner and in line for a promotion to management supervisor in the near future. But as Pete was leaving work one night, he overheard several of the other account people talking about someone who "was lucky" and who "couldn't say no to that opportunity." His heart sank when he realized that it was Carol they were talking about, and that she had accepted a job at another ad agency. A mandatory agency meeting had been scheduled for 8:00 a.m. the next morning, and Pete was sure that in addition to announcing Carol's departure, the agency would announce her replacement. Pete was anxious to hear whom he would be reporting to after Carol left.

The next morning, over coffee and bagels, it was announced that Carol was leaving and that her replacement, Ted Sands, had been hired from an out-of-town ad agency. Ted's qualifications seemed solid, his formal education was impressive, and he had working experience at several major ad agencies. The management at Brunner made it sound like the transition from Carol to Ted would be seamless, and that the clients were "all aboard." Although Pete was disappointed that he would not get to work with Carol, he had every expectation that his new boss would be just fine. In fact, a dinner to welcome Ted was scheduled for the following week. Pete was looking forward to it.

TED

After four weeks, Pete was starting to wonder about Ted's management style. Ted had a brusque, direct style. He appeared to be a "workaholic," often staying at the agency late into the night. He didn't socialize much, saying he didn't want to get to know the others too well, "in case he had to fire them." No one was sure if it was said as a joke. Pete also observed that Ted doled out more criticism than praise, and he never seemed to accept the blame for anything. But the part that had Pete frustrated and concerned was Ted's poor communication skills. Ted didn't give clear directions to his team, and he bristled when asked a question that he thought he had already answered. He didn't take the time to train the team as Carol would have, and he was constantly bad-mouthing team members. Pete thought, "If Ted is telling me why Brenda and Rob are so stupid, what is he telling them about me?"

Still new to the job and the agency, Pete decided this was just another challenge that he would master, the same way he had mastered the course material at State University.

STATE UNIVERSITY'S ADVERTISING CLUB

While Pete was a student at State University, he had been very active in the Advertising Club, the student-run campus organization made up mostly of students majoring in advertising. One of the features of the club that the membership loved was its ability to attract talented professionals as guest speakers. These speakers gave the students a look into the inside working of the advertising and marketing community, and in many instances they supported with their experience the same things the outstanding faculty taught in the classroom. These meetings also gave students the opportunity to network with practicing professionals and get noticed for internships or jobs after college.

In one of Pete's recent conversations with a friend who was still at the university, his friend mentioned that the Ad Club had invited Stan Chandler as its next guest speaker. Chandler, a managing partner at Big Frog Creative Studio, had spent more than

25 years in advertising, marketing, and design, and he was an adjunct faculty member at several local universities. He had spoken many times on the topic "A Profile of Successful Advertising People," and Pete had never heard him speak, so he was eager to attend the club's next meeting.

Pete wondered if anything he would hear at the Ad Club would give him insight into what made his new account supervisor tick.

STAN CHANDLER'S PRESENTATION TO THE AD CLUB

"Thanks for inviting me to speak to you. I love to be in the presence of bright, motivated future advertising superstars. The advertising business has always attracted interesting people, and that is why I've liked it so much for the past 25 years. It is generally a business of 'young' people, although there are places and positions where senior talent is appreciated and needed. It is a business of ideas, and the best ideas generally win. Because good ideas do not rely on physical attributes, and because good ideas are not gender specific, almost anyone who is willing to work hard, work smart, and be a creative thinker can be successful in the advertising business.

"Now, you may think I am just referring to artwork, or design, when I talk about creativity. I am not. Creative thinking is needed and a necessary part of almost everything we do in the advertising business, whether it's in media planning or buying, research, public relations work, account service work, or management.

"It has been my contention for a long time that clients do not want to buy ads or brochures. Or design. Or collateral materials. What they want is a solution to a business problem or a response to an opportunity that is in front of them. They look at what we do as providing a means for a solution that happens to be in the shape of an ad, or brochure, or design. If an agency or designer does not fulfill the need for a creative solution, then the work they do is of little value to a client. Note I say 'to a client,' because most ad agency art directors or designers pour their hearts and talents into everything they do. Or at least they should. It is time for these artists to realize that artistic excellence and marketing effectiveness may not be one and the same.

"The idea of 'pouring your heart into something' is a trait that is very common among creative thinkers. Remember, I am not just talking about artists. In advertising agencies, this trait is usually defined as 'passion.' Passion for the ad business is reflected in the account executive that is relentless in staying current on his client's business. Passion is reflected by the late-night reading a media planner does to keep current on changes and options in the world of media. Passion for the business can also be defined as intensity when it counts, a restlessness that says work can always be better, and a willingness—actually 'desire' is a better word—to come up with the best, most cost-effective solution in the time available. Most of the people that practice 'great advertising' have never even heard of a 40-hour workweek, much less experienced one.

"It is not unusual for people in our business to be good communicators. Often, an idea is only as good as your ability to express it and convince others of its brilliance. Many of us love to 'be on stage' and present ideas, and often successful people in this business have an element of 'show biz' in them when it comes to making a presentation. This business attracts independent, confident people who believe in their abilities. It is not at all uncommon to have all traits wrapped in a strong personality.

"To be successful in this business you must be a self-starter, but you must also be able to ask for help. You have to be a good presenter, but skills as a great listener can also take you far. You have to know when to ask for permission, and when to ask for forgiveness. You have to be not only able to defend your ideas, but *willing* to do it at the drop of a hat, while looking forward to it. You must be motivated by achievement, but not so motivated by personal gain as to think you can do it alone.

"In other words, successful people in the advertising business seem to have a somewhat rare combination of left-brain and right-brain thinking wrapped in a strong personality and topped with self-confidence and passion."

Stan Chandler then ended his talk by saying, "Some of my opinions and observations might be slightly off the mark. But not by much. If you are lucky enough to work in this business after graduation, I'm confident that you will find most of what I have said to be true. Again, thank you for inviting me to speak with you this evening."

Pete reflected on Stan's comments in light of his relationship with his account supervisor. Had he heard anything that might give him insights about Ted? Could he use any of Stan's observations, gained over 25 years, to improve his working relationship with Ted?

QUESTIONS

1. What do you think of Stan's remarks?
2. Which of Stan's remarks told you something you didn't know? Which of Stan's remarks told you something you already knew?
3. Do you think Stan's remarks are accurate? What would you disagree with?
4. Do you think people who work in advertising are really different from everyone else?
5. Which observations made by Stan seem to apply most directly to Ted?
6. What should Pete do? What would you do?

PART V

Summary Cases

About the Summary Cases

THIS PART OF the text represents a unique departure from many case textbooks. Cases 41–46 are provided to help students review and categorize the learnings from the previous case materials in a meaningful way. Cases 41–45 provide an overview of four dimensions that form the world of advertising and marketing management: the tools, the people, the programs, and the jobs that are available, while case 46 looks at the future of advertising and marketing. Many of the details and specifics of these cases were presented individually in the cases in the preceding parts of this book. Key learning points are reviewed in the summary cases presented here, and additional questions are provided to build a more complete understanding of each area.

It is important to understand the complexity and ever changing nature of advertising and marketing. Often students come to a management course having been exposed to some of the functional tools in their field of interest, whether it is advertising or marketing. Yet the people (case 42), and the programs (case 43) that are such a necessary element in order for the tools (case 41) to work have not been integrated into their thinking. This section seeks to provide that integration. Further, it provides a means to tie together the 40 individual cases of this book into a course experience that replicates the realities of today's business world.

One thing that seems certain about the future of advertising and marketing is that these fields, especially advertising, will continue to change and evolve as they have done since the advent of television in the early 1950s. Within the advertising and marketing community, 2005 may be remembered as a "watershed" year. In 2005 more money was spent by individuals on products and services to avoid seeing and hearing advertising (TiVo, iPods, video on demand, DVD movies) than was spent by advertisers buying network television time to show it. The future of advertising and marketing will certainly be interesting.

The Tools of Advertising and Marketing Management

THE TOOLS OF advertising and marketing management are the techniques, materials, media, and deliverables that managers use to solve marketing- and advertising-related problems. Sometimes, rather than being used to solve a problem, these tools are employed to meet an opportunity or capitalize on an advantage.

Before any of the tools are used, a manager must evaluate the situation and identify one or more objectives and one or more strategies. A manager must think about the tactics most likely to successfully meet the objectives. Sometimes a formal process is in place to do this for large marketing projects or major advertising campaigns. The creative brief introduced in the **McNair & Company** case is an example of this. Analyses such as those described in the **PEST, SWOT, and the Crafts Company** case are other examples. But even if the situation or opportunity does not call for or allow a formal approach, good marketing and advertising managers do these evaluations instinctively.

The advantage of thinking in an organized way is that it allows a manager to quickly eliminate certain tools, and it allows for focusing on the tools that will work best to accomplish the objectives. The **Bank of Ayden** case looks at marketing and advertising tools in a small market. **Neptune Aquatic Club** asks if the same tools used by for-profit companies will work for a nonprofit organization. The **Polk, Fales & Crumley Advertising** case examines what it is like when an advertising agency seemingly runs out of energy and ideas that might result in new or more effective tools. The **PizzaTown, Inc.** case concentrates on the use of media tools to address a marketing need.

One of the tools that is often overlooked is research. The **Segmenting, Targeting, Positioning (STP) and Here's to Your Health Frozen Dinners** case describes the importance of research. The case about **Consumer Buying Behavior and the Plumber**

Clothing Company is another that focuses on research. Once a manager has taken a look at objectives and strategy, and after research has been done, he or she can then begin to look at tactics and the tools to meet the objectives.

Message strategy and copy testing can be done as communications are crafted. The case about **Venus Motor Sales** depicts the vice president of marketing's concerns about the company's advertising message. If the situation is retail related, then a manager might look at sales promotion ideas. The **AA Motorcycles** case discusses the use of a sales promotion to promote the brand. Or perhaps the need is for in-store point-of-purchase materials, which are discussed in the case on **P-O-P Advertising and the Taylor Advertising Agency**.

Large clients and their respective advertising agencies are developing what is called "integrated marketing communications campaigns." These campaigns use various media to present messages about products or services. The case about the **Marshall Company** describes its agency's efforts to provide a seamless message using several media.

And lastly, there are tools available that have not been the subject of a case in this book. Yet they are no less important than the ones you have read. The list is long, but the following tools are used every day:

- Public relations
- Database marketing
- Product placement
- Trade shows
- Guerrilla marketing
- Contests and sweepstakes
- Unique packaging
- Sales and discounts
- Continuity and rewards programs
- Direct marketing

QUESTIONS

1. Which of the tools of advertising and marketing management do you think is the most effective? Why?
2. Besides cost, what are some of the most commonly encountered obstacles to using all of the tools available?
3. Which tool impresses you the most? Why?
4. What is guerrilla marketing?
5. What are some of the tools of public relations?
6. Find an example of "unique packaging" and bring it to class. Do you think the packaging helps make the sale?

7. When is a trade show an effective tool?
8. Bring a product to class and discuss what research may have told the manufacturer or seller about you, the customer?
9. Is Internet marketing just a fad? Why, or why not?
10. Which case about the tools of advertising and marketing management is your favorite? Why? What did you learn that stands out the most?

The People in Advertising and Marketing Management

I **N GENERAL,** certain professions attract certain kinds of people. While it is also true that certain professions can change an individual's personality somewhat, the former statement is probably truer.

People can easily distinguish the great ad agencies from the also-rans. And a great ad agency's real assets leave every day when their work is done. Clients want to hire agencies that employ smart people—people with passion, a point of view, and a willingness to think in nontraditional terms.

Imagine for a moment that an ad agency is a basketball team. They're in a tough game, are down by one point, have the ball, and have just called a time out with 10 seconds to go. It's likely the coach would say, "OK, here's the situation. We need a basket when time resumes, or we will lose this game. We don't need a three-pointer, just a two-point basket or a foul so we can get the chance to shoot two free throws to win. I've got a play in mind for that final shot. Who wants to take it?"

Most of the players would say, "I'll take it." Similarly, ad agencies attract confident, optimistic individuals who have often been successful in many past activities. Most players would think that they could make the final shot for the win. Most would be willing to risk being the "hero" or the "goat," depending on whether the game was won or lost. Actually, most wouldn't be able to resist the opportunity to be that hero! Why? Because they'd be thinking, "If I shoot it, it will go in." Period.

When that final shot is taken, if it *doesn't* go in, the shooter will likely be surprised and probably think, "I can't believe it didn't go in!" Not, "I missed the shot." Rather, "I can't believe it didn't go in!" The latter reflects a confidence, an expectation for success, and a surprise that the situation didn't turn out as it should have.

This attitude, often a bit edgy, often nontraditional, often unconventional and controversial, is what makes many of the people in advertising what they are. And it is also what makes going to work in an advertising agency each day fun, exciting, a challenge, and a new adventure.

Some of the positive sides of this "ad agency personality" are seen in the **McNair & Company**, **Harrison Advertising**, and **2 Guys and a Girl** cases. Unfortunately, some of the downsides to an aggressive, driven personality are on display in the **Perkins Advertising**, **Design Circus**, **Polk, Fales & Crumley Advertising**, and **Pete Boswell, Account Executive** cases.

Strong personalities are not exclusive to ad agencies. Often clients possess the same positives and negatives of a strong personality. This is seen in the **Benson Machine Company**, **West Greenville Convention and Visitors Bureau**, and **PizzaTown, Inc.** cases. Other glimpses at personality profiles of some of the people in advertising and marketing are seen in the **Museum Board of the State of California**, **Smith Services**, and **Norman Surgical Supply Company** cases.

No single approach to solving marketing and advertising challenges is appropriate for all companies or ad agencies. Each company has its own personality and culture. Often that personality is driven by the product or service the company sells, or by the part of the country in which it is located. Sometimes it is the result of a tone set by the person who founded the company. Sometimes it is the result of who manages the company today.

Regardless, when looking at situations in marketing or advertising, it is almost always appropriate and wise to consider, explore, and understand "the people factor."

- Who stands to win or lose from a pending decision?
- What is the history of the people involved?
- Where have they worked before?
- Whom do they report to?
- Where did they go to school?
- Where are they from?

Newcomers to advertising and marketing often display a surprising lack of "people planning." Crucial questions they should contemplate before any internal or external meetings are:

- Who will be at the meeting? Why?
- Who is the *real* leader of the meeting?
- Who stands to gain from a certain decision?
- Who stands to lose?
- What will people's personal agendas be?

Quite often, when someone is asked to leave an ad agency, it is not because he or she has been unable to do the job; it is because the person does not fit into the agency's culture. This culture can be the result of many things. But people—past or present—are generally behind most of them.

To be a successful advertising or marketing professional, you must know how to perform the duties and tasks that are necessary for a specific job, but your success will hinge in large measure on how adept you are in managing "the people factor."

QUESTIONS

1. Do you think the hiring process at an ad agency should be any different from that of any other kind of business? Why, or why not?
2. If you were an interviewer, what would be the most important thing you should learn from a candidate for a marketing or advertising job?
3. As an interviewee, is there any one thing you think *must* be communicated to a prospective employer? Explain.
4. What can an applicant's cover letter tell you?
5. What do you think about pre-employment testing? What testing is permissible? (This question requires some research that can easily be done online.)
6. Where would you go to recruit candidates for your ad agency?
7. Advertising agencies and marketing companies want people who think "outside the box." Do you think this means you can act "outside the box" in trying to get a job at one of these companies? Explain.
8. For extra credit, interview a personnel manager who hires advertising or marketing talent. Write a 2–3 page report on what kind of person the manager looks for, and the kind of person that generally succeeds in advertising or marketing.

The Programs Used in Advertising and Marketing Management

THERE ARE MANY programs used in the management of marketing and advertising activity. By "programs," we mean structured approaches to addressing marketing and advertising issues that employ multilayered tactics or multiple marketing and advertising tools.

Five of the most commonly used programs are:

1. Discovery and research.
2. A marketing plan.
3. A sales forecast or budget.
4. An integrated marketing communications (IMC) plan.
5. A pure advertising campaign.

DISCOVERY AND RESEARCH

A discovery and research program is the ideal way to begin the process of building a solution to a marketing problem or opportunity. Often, small companies or individuals do not have the time or resources to do this in a formal way. But with experience, many managers do this informally and instinctively.

Discovery involves asking questions in face-to-face meetings with clients or staff, doing research on the Internet, doing competitive research, asking the client for any research that is available on the subject in question, visiting the client's location, talking to others in the client's organization, talking to competitors, talking to customers, and talking to noncustomers. Discovery is just what it says—a series of investigations to learn all you can before action is taken. Quite often it can be done for only the investment of time, obtaining secondary research from already available sources.

In order to get the most from discovery, an investigator must be well prepared, knowing the questions to be asked and having a well-thought-out focus for what he or she is trying to find out. Questioning should be drawn from a set of learning objectives that are prioritized based on their importance to the project.

In a pure research approach, researchers often gather information in a completely neutral way, allowing the data to shape the finding. The outcome from that data may or may not surprise the researcher. From this data and investigation, the researcher then prepares a report of the findings. Often this is where the researcher's job ends.

In marketing and advertising management, experience has taught that it is better to approach discovery with a point of view that the manager has formed *before* the discovery begins. In this way, the questioning can be more focused, and the answers can be placed in a business decision-making context. And, while a report or position paper may result, it is often someone at the ad agency who will have to present the findings and conclusions, usually in person, and usually to a large and senior audience. For discovery to be effective, the *data* gathered must be turned into *information*, and that information then turned into *insight*. Insight, not data or information, is what is most usable in business decision making. Effective marketing or advertising strategy deals with the opportunity, not the problem. It is with this in mind that discovery should be undertaken.

Primary research, as the second part of the discovery process, often follows discovery. Since discovery just involves secondary research and informal conversations with as many people as are appropriate, it may be necessary to move to primary research for more specific answers. Primary research is a customized look into discovery. Usually, a research firm is engaged to design the research instrument, or questionnaire, and it is this same research firm that should be asked what type of research is best suited for the answers sought.

Primary research can be categorized as qualitative or quantitative. Qualitative research is directional in nature, often suggesting trends or general findings. When it is presented, you will probably hear words like "usually," "generally," "mostly," or "it seems." A marketing or advertising manager may take this formal step to engage primary qualitative research to confirm suspicions or discovery findings, or it may be to bring a neutral, unbiased third party to the table. Clients generally have more faith and confidence in non-agency-produced research than in the kind an agency researcher might do.

Quantitative research is numbers oriented. It seeks to put hard edges on questions and report the results in terms of absolute numbers, percentages, indices, averages, means, and modes. Quantitative research is great for data and information. It becomes more usable when the question "What does that *mean?*" is addressed and studied.

Again, the value of discovery and any following research, whether it's qualitative or quantitative, or obtained from telephone interviews or focus groups, is the *insight* that results from what is gathered.

Discovery and research is the process that Will Jackson went through to gain insight in the **McNair & Company** case. Chris Harrison used the process informally in the

Harrison Advertising case, and it most certainly came into play in the **Bank of Ayden** and **Neptune Aquatic Club** cases.

A MARKETING PLAN

A marketing plan is a broad set of guidelines as to how a company is going to accomplish its strategic goals and a blueprint for future marketing activity. It is a coordinated, integrated outline of everything that will be done by the company in each of its marketing functions—such as research, planning, advertising, public relations, sales promotion, direct marketing, sales management, product development, pricing, and distribution management—to support the company's purpose and strategic business plan.

A marketing plan states what will be done, who will do it, when it will be done, why it will be done, and how much it will cost. In the case of a marketing plan, cost refers to personnel, facilities, and doing business.

While individual marketing plans differ, they often have key common elements. Most marketing plans will likely include:

- A situation analysis.
- Marketing objectives.
- Marketing strategies.
- Tactics.
- A means of evaluation.

Typically, a situation analysis examines such internal and external factors as current marketing operations and activities, what the competition is doing, and what is going on in the marketplace where the company competes. Sometimes the format of this analysis is described by the acronym SWOT: the company takes a look at its strengths, weaknesses, opportunities, and threats. The case on **PEST, SWOT, and the Crafts Company** describes a SWOT Analysis and how it can be useful in business.

Marketing objectives, or goals, are based on the conclusions and insights gained from the situation analysis. Usually, they are general in scope and are written to identify a path that the company will take toward its strategic objectives.

Marketing strategies describe *how* the marketing goals will be approached, and generally each goal or objective has a related, specific strategy. Tactics describe very specific, detailed actions that must be taken to implement each strategy. Well-thought-out tactics should include an identification of what is to be done, who is responsible, a timeframe for action, and a budget to get it done.

Usually, a marketing plan includes an identification of how success will be measured. What will be evaluated? When will the evaluation be done?

While almost everyone in marketing or advertising acknowledges the value of and need for a thorough marketing plan, the degree to which plans are produced is not universal. There are many excellent texts devoted specifically to how to create and prepare a marketing plan. Most marketing textbooks provide a much more detailed look at this fundamental marketing program than has been presented here.

A SALES FORECAST OR BUDGET

Quite often, preparing a sales forecaset or budget is one of the first steps taken by an organization as it begins or plans for a new fiscal year. In most advertising agencies, the forecast is generally "an educated guess," because while an agency can identify what it expects or hopes an existing client will spend in the coming year, it really doesn't know. When you add to this the unknowns of new business acquisition (**West Greenville Convention and Visitors Bureau**), the economy, lost clients (**Harrison Advertising**), and bad creative decisions (**Museum Board of the State of California**), an accurate forecast of sales (agency billings) is difficult to make.

Yet every ad agency needs a number that represents how much it thinks it will issue invoices for, or bill for the coming year. Based on historical trends, it can then reduce this gross billings number to a gross income number by subtracting the cost-of-sales amount. Gross income is what will be available to pay salaries and other expenses such as rent, insurance, benefits, and supplies. After these expenses are met, any gross income left then becomes net income, or profit (see the cases on **Smith Services**, **Benson Machine Company**, and **Norman Surgical Supply Company**).

At Locomotion Creative, a branding and design company located in Nashville, Tennessee, account management people are asked, quarterly, to report what they think their clients will spend for the remaining months of the year. To this total is added new business acquired in the past months of the same fiscal year and a figure for any likely new business that is in active discussion. This new sales total and then the resulting gross income figure are used to forecast where management thinks the company will end the year. The gross income figure is also the basis for decisions regarding personnel, equipment purchases, and overall expenses for the remaining months of the year.

While there is always an element of "guess" in any forecast, many marketing organizations make extensive use of computer modeling to produce sales forecasts for the coming year. Quite often, forecasting is done beyond one year into the future. This is especially true for companies in capital-intensive industries or those that operate internationally. The case about the **Koch Brewing Company** describes the marketing director's responsibilities, including developing short-term and long-term sales forecasts.

Imagine the complexity of trying to plan sales at a company like Exxon-Mobil. The building of refineries or production capacity is a very expensive proposition, not to mention the time delay for construction and to get all necessary Environmental Protection Agency approvals. Then there is the oil supply question, driven in no small degree by OPEC, the Organization of Petroleum Exporting Countries. Add to this currency shifts and political instability around the world, which can affect both costs and revenues, and it is easy to see that just arriving at a sales number, even if it is based on past volume, is "challenging." Yet, just as at Locomotion Creative, it must be done as accurately as possible.

Most industries have their own customized means of sales forecasting and budgeting (see the **Koch Brewing Company** case). However, in most cases, no matter how complex it is, or how long it takes, or how many people are involved, the process is an imperfect blend of art and science.

INTEGRATED MARKETING COMMUNICATIONS

Much has been written about integrated marketing communications (IMC). It is very difficult to argue against the logic of having all messaging and marketing tactics be consistent across many media. This has been the goal of most ad agencies for years, and paradoxically, it has generally been smaller agencies that have been able to pull it off more successfully than large, multinational agencies.

The term "integrated marketing communications" has been attached to many authors, but the concept originated at a large Madison Avenue ad agency in New York City. Noticing that the television advertising they were doing for a major client didn't resemble the out-of-home advertising being done by another client vendor, and also that the key message was different, the agency positioned itself as a coordinating source for message consistency. In this way, they argued, all client communications can "speak in one voice," and the accumulated weight and impact of repetition in look and content, spread over many media (radio, TV, magazine, newspaper, etc.), would do a better, more efficient job of communicating for the client. Further, they positioned themselves as not just a producer of ads, but as a valuable resource to integrate all communications for the benefit of their clients.

Since then, the jury has been out on whether IMC provides what was promised, or whether such an integration was even possible in the first place. Smaller ad agencies seem able to do it because, with smaller clients that are not trying for a national market, they naturally provide *everything* the small client needs: ads, PR, collateral materials, P-O-P, and so forth. For larger clients, agencies are used to going to specialty vendors for needs beyond ads. For example, they may hire a public relations firm that is different from the firm creating collateral materials, which is a different firm from the one that creates and provides in-store fixturing and point-of-sale materials.

With so many firms involved, however, conflicts over resources, differing opinions as to which medium is the most important, and vendor egos often lead to messaging and execution that may be greatly or slightly different from all the others for the brand or product. At this point, the ad agency is no longer able to control the integration of marketing communications, and it becomes the client's responsibility. And if the client thinks all is going well with each medium, or if campaign objectives are being achieved, the client may not want to tinker with success.

Thus, academics and ad agency people have declared that IMC either works well or is a bust. Actually, the degree to which IMC has been successfully implemented depends on whom you ask.

The **Marshall Company** case describes an advertising agency's integrated marketing communications campaign for the Marshall Company's D. G. Jeans. Both the **Bank of Ayden** and **Neptune Aquatic Club** cases are examples of two clients that are ideal candidates for an IMC approach.

A TRADITIONAL AGENCY-GENERATED AD CAMPAIGN

Probably the place where the agency-generated ad campaign is practiced the most is on Madison Avenue in New York City. Madison Avenue is the traditional home of many multinational ad agencies. In many ways, "Madison Avenue" has come to symbolize the way things are done in advertising. But smaller, more nimble ad agencies like Mad Dogs and Englishmen or kirshenbaum bond + partners in New York have been turning out great work at addresses other than Madison Avenue. The same goes for Crispin Porter + Bogusky, in Miami. And there are many more.

Regardless of where it takes place, a traditional ad agency advertising campaign has the following elements:

- Possibly a new client (see **West Greenville Convention and Visitors Bureau**).
- A media component (see **PizzaTown, Inc.**).
- An ad agency (see **Polk, Fales & Crumley**).
- A creative brief (see **McNair & Company**).

Probably the most complete example of the process, events, and emotions that transpire in creating an advertising campaign can be seen in the **Museum Board of the State of California** case.

An advertising campaign is a multipart communications effort aimed at a specific target audience. The traditional advertising campaign is built around media advertising, often using all of the media classes available: television (broadcast and cable), print (magazines and newspapers), perhaps direct mail, interactive marketing, out-of-home advertising, radio, the Internet, and nontraditional venues. Generally, the driving creative execution for these campaigns has been the television creative. This has been true for many years, but now the unique attributes of other media are often leading to modifications of the television creative. Each medium has its own strengths and weaknesses. Today's smart ad agencies are taking full advantage of this and are not trying to force television creative into all media.

The objective of an advertising campaign is to use multiple tools to reach the target audience. Each time the "message" is presented to that target can be considered a possible "impression"—possible, because reaching a target audience doesn't mean they will hear, see, or even notice your message. Because of the "iffy-ness" of message reception and recognition, a campaign seeks to bombard the target with as many impressions and repetitions as possible.

What must be kept in mind is that most ad campaign objectives have an underlying business basis. Campaigns should not be seen solely as opportunities for the agency to win awards, or as revenue-producing vehicles. In most cases, if advertising campaigns do not help clients move their business forward, there is a good chance that the ad agency will be replaced. The ramifications of an agency losing business can be clearly seen in the **Harrison Advertising** case.

An advertising campaign from a mid-sized or bigger ad agency is part science and part art. It is rational and emotional. It is based on facts that are then polished to get recognition. All campaigns contain some measure of research and intuition. And because many advertising campaigns are evolving, organic creatures, they sometimes take on a life of their own. This has led to many spectacular failures, agency awards, and agency firings. Among the most notable are past campaigns for Taco Bell, Mercury, Hardee's, and Miller Beer.

At the end of the day, advertising campaigns are created by people—which is what makes the creation and selling of an advertising campaign both fascinating and frustrating at the same time. No other business is as much work and fun as advertising.

QUESTIONS

1. Make some notes about an advertising campaign that you like that is currently running. Why do you like it? Why do you think it is effective? Would others react to it the way you do? Be prepared to discuss the campaign.
2. Would you add other "programs" to those identified in this summary case?
3. What factors drive the degree to which discovery is pursued?
4. What is the objective of research?
5. What is psychographic research? How accurate do you think it is?
6. Do you agree that an advertising or marketing manager should have a point of view before discovery begins? Why, or why not?
7. Turn *data* into *information*, and then turn information into *insight*. What does this mean? What is your definition of insight?
8. What are your thoughts on the advice that effective marketing or advertising strategy should deal with the opportunity rather than the problem?
9. Given the kinds of personalities in advertising and marketing, is integrated marketing communications a realistic concept? Do you think IMC works?
10. Are the days of "advertising campaigns" over? Explain.
11. Do a little Internet research on Crispin Porter + Bogusky, kirshenbaum bond + partners, and Mad Dogs and Englishmen. What did you find? How are these agencies alike? What is your overall conclusion about what you learned about them?
12. How is the "people factor" reflected in advertising campaigns?
13. What is a "great" advertising campaign?

Jobs at Advertising Agencies

THROUGHOUT THE cases of this book, you have met individuals, either real or fictional, who work in advertising or marketing management. In this summary case, we look at some of the jobs in advertising that have appeared in this text, along with others in the field. In the next summary case, we will look at some of the jobs available in marketing.

ACCOUNT MANAGEMENT JOBS

Administrative Assistant (AA)

This job is generally a detail-oriented, clerical-type job. While there may be some client contact, generally it is this person's job to keep track of client contact reports and correspondence with the wide range of people that an account executive works with, both inside and outside the agency. Often, the administrative assistant may be tasked with monitoring client budgets managed by the agency. An agency may or may not require a college degree for the AA position. The successful AA is someone who is organized and can stay that way, someone who is flexible in tasking, someone with tact and social skills, and someone who probably gets too little credit. This job can be an entry-level opportunity for a college graduate to get into ad agency account management.

Assistant Account Executive (AAE)

This job is another typical entry point for new hires in the ad agency account management world. It differs from the AA position because the AAE usually interacts with staffers at the client company. If the account executive for whom the AAE works also works on another account, the AAE will take client calls, open jobs, keep the client informed, be the client's portal to the agency in the account executive's absence, and generally perform as a short-term account executive.

This job requires the ability to be a good listener, to be an accomplished multitasker, and to have telephone and superior writing skills. This is not a 40-hour-a-week job. Late hours will be needed to support the account executive you work for. As an AAE, you must be able to get things done, and you must be aware of the budget and estimates as you work. You will be expected to keep track of client work at the agency and when it is due. You will also be expected to work profitably as an agency team member. Successful performance will earn you a shot at an account executive position.

Bob Smith, in the **Perkins Advertising** case, is an assistant account executive.

Account Executive (AE)

An AE is the frontline foot soldier at all ad agencies. He or she is the primary contact with the client and is responsible for building a relationship with the client that is professional and personal. The AE conducts meetings with the client to get assignments and then makes the agency's presentation to the client after the agency has added value to each job. The added value might take many shapes: a media plan, a public relations assignment, an ad, or a broadcast message. Good AEs figure out what the client needs and then get the rest of the agency focused to deliver it profitably. Imagine the AE as the hub of a wheel, interacting with the creative department, the media department, research, public relations, finance, and so forth. AEs have to be generalists who can answer the first five questions a client has on any aspect of the agency operation. They have to provide marketing *leadership* to clients of all experience levels.

As is the case with every job at most ad agencies, this job is absolutely gender neutral. Successful AEs have to be able to multitask, know how business works, and *know everything they can about the client and the client's business*. They need to have a restrained aggressiveness about them to get things done. They have to be smart and curious yet understanding and confident. Good AEs are not just order takers or delivery people. They understand the client's business, and they have a point of view on what it will take to make the client successful. An ad agency without really strong account executives is doomed to mediocrity.

Examples of account executives are Angela Graham in the **Museum Board of the State of California** case, and Pete Boswell in **Pete Boswell, Account Executive**.

Account Supervisor (AS)

On a large account, an AS will manage multiple AEs. At smaller agencies, an AS might also manage multiple AEs, but they might be working on different clients. A good AE gets promoted to an AS.

Tom Huang, in the **Museum Board of the State of California** case, is an account supervisor, as is Carol Lipscomb in **Pete Boswell, Account Executive**.

Management Supervisor (MS)

The job level above the account supervisor is the account management supervisor. Management supervisors manage multiple account supervisors.

Account Manager (AM)

At some ad agencies the account manager title is used for an entry-level position. At most agencies, however, it describes the *one* person in charge of a large agency account. This is often a senior ad agency person who interacts on an executive level with the highest-level contacts at the agency client. Account managers get to be account managers because they have worked up the chain from an entry-level account management position, have demonstrated superior advertising and business skills, are politically savvy, are socially talented, and conduct themselves with confidence and authority.

Fran Franzini in the **McNair & Company** case is an account manager.

Vice President or Director of Client Services

This individual has overall responsibility for all of the agency's client relationships. VPs and directors are generally very strategic in their thinking, experienced in working with a varied client base, have experience in the major categories of business an agency might find itself working in (financial services, health care, retail, business-to-business, etc.), and possess strong verbal and written skills. At many agencies, this person is responsible for new business development and acquisition. This is a well-paying, demanding, reward-ing, pressure-packed, long-hours job. Not many people get offered this position.

See the **West Greenville Convention and Visitors Bureau** case.

Researcher, Account Planner, Brand Architect

All three of these positions, or variations on them, are generally available at most mid-sized to large ad agencies. A researcher gathers data and conducts studies that are designed by an account planner.

An account planner is charged with becoming "the voice of the consumer." It is the account planner's role to search for *insight* among the data and information that the researcher gathers. This insight comes only when the consumer's, or prospect's, inner-most feelings and desires are understood, as they relate to a product or service. What is the most important motivating factor when buying *X*? What is the consumer really buy-ing? What obvious and below the surface needs does the product or service meet?

The researcher's information and the account planner's insight can then lead to a more effective strategy to cause the consumer or prospect to take action (see **McNair & Company**).

The brand architect position is most often found at ad agencies that work for large consumer goods companies (such as Procter & Gamble, Nabisco, Miller Beer). A brand architect is charged with building, maintaining, and expanding the meaning and value of a brand. When should positioning be changed? What activities are appropriate for a brand? What line extensions or new products can be added to the brand that will not diminish or cheapen the brand's equity? How can a new brand be built and introduced?

Part researcher, part account planner, and part social scientist, a brand architect is a valuable player at today's ad agencies as clients face competition from in-house brands, such as those found at Kroger, Wal-Mart, and Home Depot.

CREATIVE JOBS

Copywriter

The starting point of tangible creativity at an ad agency is often with copywriters. By tangible, we mean output that the client will see. Once the researcher and account planner have done their parts, the copywriter will begin to draft words that become "the message." If an agency is well managed, this message will be the result of a well-written creative brief that "frames" the situation, allowing the copywriter to concentrate on the essential elements that need to be communicated. The copywriter crafts the message; the art director makes it noticeable.

Copywriters come from varied backgrounds. Sometimes they have degrees in English; sometimes they learn the trade from a school such as Creative Circus, in Atlanta. If writing and words have not been your thing in the past, and you do not have a portfolio of past work to show, it is almost impossible to get hired as a copywriter. The best way to become a copywriter is to talk to an agency copywriter and see how that person did it. As with most ad agency creative department jobs, you either are or aren't a candidate based on *past, relevant creative experience*.

Art Director (AD), Production Artist

An ad agency art director, often working with a copywriter, is responsible for adding the visual component to the message. If the content—the message—is to be noticed, read, and understood, then a differentiating, arresting, and interesting visual component must be added. This can take the form of a four-color magazine print ad, a black-and-white newspaper ad, an out-of-home advertising message, a TV spot, or any number of new and emerging delivery vehicles such as streaming video, branded entertainment, or website presentation. Stephen Miles in the **Museum Board of the State of California** case is an art director.

At larger agencies, a production artist will be the one who actually creates the electronic artwork that the print production manager will then produce. A production artist must be absolutely fluent in all creative software and be able to work accurately and fast.

As with a copywriter, most people who find jobs as an AD or production artist have been doing visually creative things for some time. Generally, they have had a formal introduction to design and layout through schooling, and they always have a portfolio of sample work to show. This portfolio of work is the single most important asset anyone seeking one of these positions can have. Without a strong portfolio, it will be almost impossible to get hired by any ad agency.

Creative Director (CD)

The creative director might have been an associate creative director (ACD) before assuming this top position. Almost certainly, he or she has been a successful, award-winning copywriter or art director. The CD is the final voice and approval source for all creative work that leaves the ad agency. In addition to managing all the copywriters and art directors, the CD is charged with improving their work individually and collectively, and with keeping the agency's creative output fresh and on target strategically. The CD is usually a member of the inner circle of agency senior management. Without a visionary, current, talented, well-rounded, business-savvy, serious-minded, and mature CD, most ad agencies will struggle to attract new clients or talented creative people. Without these, an ad agency cannot survive long term.

See the **Polk, Fales & Crumley Advertising** case.

Print Production Manager, Broadcast Production Manager

These are two different jobs in an ad agency. One deals with managing the production of broadcast and some electronic materials (TV spots, radio commercials, websites); the other deals with managing the production of printed materials (prints ads, collateral materials, etc.).

These are not glamorous jobs. They require incredible attention to detail and budgets. There are always time pressures for speedier delivery. Media closing dates must be met. Deliveries must be coordinated and managed. Last-minute changes or revisions must be dealt with. And, at any stage in the process, if the product is not up to agency quality standards, the production company or printer must be told in no uncertain terms, "This is not acceptable." Faced with materials that are unacceptable, the agency must then see that the situation is corrected in time to meet established deadlines. If deadlines are going to be missed, the agency (account management) must tell the client. This is not a happy situation.

Should an error be made by the agency that is not caught in proofreading or by the production people, and should the agency have to reprint a brochure or reshoot a TV commercial *at the agency's expense*, a production manager can be in serious career difficulty. It has often been said that an ad agency can lose more money in the production department in five minutes than it can make in 30 days of normal operations. Good production managers are vital to an agency's output, credibility, and profitability.

Traffic Manager

A traffic manager is responsible for the smooth flow of creative work within the agency as it moves from the account executive to the copywriter to the art director to the creative director to the account executive to the client, and back to the traffic manager. This may occur several times as the client changes and finally approves the agency's creative output. It is the traffic manager who must keep it all moving, knowing that the work must then be produced by a production manager in time to meet media closing dates or broadcast air dates. The same pressures also apply to other collateral materials that might be due for a client sales meeting or trade show.

A good traffic manager packs a "velvet hammer." He or she must be able to coax or demand the movement of creative work in an ad agency to meet internal and external deadlines. A client will not understand if it is the agency's fault that a deadline was missed. When this happens, there is generally enough blame to go around. If work sat too long in a copywriter's or art director's office because of the traffic manager's inattention or lack or forcefulness, the traffic manager may have taken his or her first step toward unemployment. This is a vital—and tough—job at any ad agency.

JOBS IN THE MEDIA DEPARTMENT

Media Planner, Media Buyer

In a larger ad agency, these are separate jobs; in most smaller agencies, one person performs both tasks. Media planning involves recommending the most effective and efficient ways, within a budget, to reach a targeted audience with the client's message. A planner usually has access to sophisticated software and tools to match media delivery vehicles with the target's lifestyle habits. Traditional tools include TV, print, radio, out-of-home advertising, direct mail, and the Internet. By the time you read this summary case, the world of media choices will have expanded geometrically and will pose additional challenges for planners trying to reach identified target audiences (see case 46, **What Is the Future for Advertising and Marketing?**).

Good media planners are detail oriented, curious, energetic, overworked, always short of time, and indispensable to agency success. They are also budget minded, creative in what they do, good presenters, and must be willing to be measured in what they do. If a client does not get the hoped-for sales increase from an advertising campaign, maybe it was because the media plan had faults. Maybe the plan was built around yesterday's media thinking. Maybe it was a subpar product or had noncompetitive pricing. Maybe it had poor distribution or unattractive packaging. In any event, it is likely that the ad agency will get at least partial blame for its creative materials or media plan.

Once a plan has been approved internally and externally, the media buyer swings into action to place the advertising and negotiate favorable costs. Since virtually all media costs are negotiable, a person in this job must be well informed about market costs and must be a skilled and tough negotiator.

Great ads or commercials are of little value if the target audience does not see them often enough. The good news for today's media planners and buyers is that media options keep growing. The bad news is that an expanded number of media options can be bewildering to ad agencies that have not kept pace with the marketplace, and this can lead to message fragmentation and poor budget choices.

A good media planner or media buyer must be a student of media on a constant basis, often keeping current through reading and studying after business hours. This is not a job for anyone who cannot multitask or is lazy. But it is one with an unlimited upside for those who figure it out. A good example is Debbie Post in the **PizzaTown** case.

Media Director

Similar to their counterparts in the account management and creative departments, media directors must manage those who do the planning and buying, and they must hire the right people, provide the right planning and buying tools, and stay ahead of the changes in new media options available. While the creative materials and the account management people are prominent features in an ad agency, it is the media department that often spends the largest percentage of a client's budget. Traditionally, 80–85 percent of the money a client spends with an ad agency is spent on media of one kind or another. Rick Blacksburg in the **PizzaTown** case is an example of a media director.

Agency Principal

A sole owner of an advertising agency, or a partner, can come from any of the functional areas previously described. He or she generally combines capability in one of those areas with an entrepreneurial spirit and the desire to "own my own company." In one ad agency, the founder and principal owner might be a former advertising manager for a fast-food company. At another ad agency, the founder and owner might be a former creative director who had been an art director earlier in his or her career. The son or daughter of an ad agency owner might decide to open an agency after gaining experience in his or her parent's agency. An agency founder might have started out as a copywriter. Or a founder could be a former director of marketing for a large corporation who moved on to become an account executive, account supervisor, and then account manager at an ad agency—and finally the owner of his or her own agency.

A common thread is drive, a solid grounding in advertising or marketing, a willingness to take a personal and financial risk, and an entrepreneurial spirit. Owners can enjoy professional and financial success, but not without having to face serious issues that only the owner of an agency can address or solve.

Examples of owners are Kelly Perkins in the **Perkins Advertising** case; Chris Harrison in **Harrison Advertising**; Jack Aaron in **Benson Machine Company**; the owners of the agencies that will present to the **West Greenville Convention and Visitors Bureau**; Victor Jay in **Smith Services**; Mike Fox in **The Design Circus**; Charles Norman in **Norman Surgical Supply**; and Elizabeth Charles in **2 Guys and a Girl**.

OTHER AD AGENCY JOBS

Ad agencies also have openings for any of the following:

Receptionist
Billing administrator
Chief financial officer
Operations manager
Information technology manager
Chief operating officer
Public relations manager

And there are others.

QUESTIONS

1. What does it take to work at an advertising agency?
2. What formal schooling is best? Explain.
3. What job or jobs appeal to you the most? How do you plan to get that job?
4. Are you willing to accept lower than average starting pay to work 50 hours or more each week in an ad agency?
5. What are some of the challenges faced by account management in the day-to-day management of their client's business?
6. What are some of the challenges creative people face in working on a client's business?
7. What are some of the challenges media people face?
8. Would you like to be an ad agency owner or partner? Explain.

Jobs in Marketing

THERE ARE NUMEROUS jobs in marketing besides those found in advertising agencies. The following descriptions cover most of the marketing positions found today in businesses and organizations in countries all over the world.

Brand Management Positions

Large consumer goods companies that manufacture or produce numerous products usually need **brand managers** who plan, develop, and direct the marketing efforts for each brand or product. A brand manager coordinates the activities of specialists in finance, research and development, purchasing, production, package development, distribution, marketing research, promotion, advertising, sales, and forecasting. Generally, a person works first as a **brand assistant**, not as a brand manager. Brand assistants have to gain experience before being promoted to brand managers. Industrial manufacturers usually need **product managers** who do basically the same jobs as brand managers.

Industrial Marketing Positions

Industrial marketing involves the planning, sale, and service of products used for commercial or business purposes. These products may be familiar items such as office supplies or complex products such as computer systems. Various positions exist, including **sales manager**, **assistant sales manager**, **sales representative**, **product manager**, **market research administrator**, **marketing manager**, and **assistant marketing manager**, among others. Generally, industrial marketing involves building a relationship between supplier and customer. Consequently, anyone who desires a position in industrial marketing must be able to help serve the needs of a variety of industrial and commercial customers on a continuing basis.

Direct Response Marketing Positions

Direct response marketing—that is, a marketer selling directly to the customer—is growing at a fast pace. Direct response media include direct mail, broadcast media, print media, telephone, catalogs, door-to-door, and e-mail, among others. Positions include **sales representative**, **sales manager**, **assistant marketing manager**, and **marketing manager**, among others.

Distribution Management Positions

Marketing logistics, or physical distribution management, includes analysis, planning, and control of activities concerned with the distribution of goods. Activities include site selection, production planning, inventory control, order processing, warehousing, and transportation. Consequently, manufacturers, trucking companies and other carriers, wholesalers, and retailers employ logistics specialists. Such positions include **distribution manager**, **inventory control manager**, **traffic manager**, **distribution center manager**, **distribution planning analyst**, and **customer service manager**.

Marketing Research Positions

Marketing research is conducted by employees within companies and by experts who work for marketing research firms. Generally, they learn about consumers, the marketing environment, and the competition. Usually, an **assistant market analyst** or **market analyst** or **market researcher** will interact with managers to identify problems and the information needed to resolve them. The assistant market analyst or market analyst designs research projects, including the data collection method and sample, conducts data analysis, prepares the reports, and presents the findings to management.

Product Planning Positions

Certain companies, especially those that produce consumer goods or services, generally have to improve old products or develop new products in order to survive in today's marketplace. **Assistant managers** or **assistant directors** of product planning or new product development need to understand marketing, research, and sales forecasting. They also need to be able to motivate others.

Retailing Management Positions

Retailers need people who are interested in merchandise management and store management, and generally the larger retailers offer formal training programs for these employees. Someone interested in merchandise management normally would progress from **assistant buyer** to **buyer** to **merchandise division manager**. Buyers are concerned with assortment selection and promotion. A person interested in store management would move from **assistant department (sales) manager** to **department manager** to **store (branch) manager**. Department managers are concerned with sales force management and display.

Sales and Sales Management Positions

For-profit and nonprofit organizations, as well as product and service organizations, need sales personnel. **Sales representatives** work for manufacturers and wholesalers who sell to other wholesalers and retailers. Generally, a sales representative will be responsible for a certain number of accounts within a specific geographic area or region. **Missionary sales representatives** typically work for manufacturers and call on retailers to persuade them to use their manufacturer's products. They tend to present persuasive information about their company's products; they do not necessarily close sales. Of course, there are other types of sales positions.

Other Positions in Marketing

In addition to the above diverse positions, people who understand marketing find employment in customer affairs, businesses that sell internationally, and purchasing.

QUESTIONS

1. For most of the positions in marketing, it is obvious that one needs to be educated in the subject. What other knowledge areas besides marketing do most of the positions require? Why?

2. Which of the above positions appeal to you? Why? Are there any that you would not desire? Why?

3. If you wanted to be a brand manager, what qualifications do you think you would need?

4. If you wanted to work in industrial marketing, which position would you choose? Why? What qualifications would this position require?

5. If you were interested in marketing research, what qualifications do you think you would need to be successful?

6. Let's say you are in charge of new product planning for Colgate-Palmolive. What educational background do you think you would need? Why?

7. What types of courses should you complete if you wanted a job in distribution management?

8. Retailers need people who have majored in marketing. Do you think you would enjoy pursuing a position in merchandise or store management? Why, or why not? What other types of courses do you think this position requires?
9. What educational background do you think you should have for a position in sales management? Why?
10. Which of the sales positions most appeals to you? Why?
11. What are three other positions in marketing that were not mentioned above? Provide a description for each.

What Is the Future for Advertising and Marketing?

AS THIS SUMMARY case is being written, most of the primary advertising trade magazines—such as *Advertising Age* and *AdWeek*—are featuring articles dealing with the question posed by the title of this case. While the trade magazines, industry observers, and those in the business will almost always answer, "It will be different," there is disagreement on what things will look like in the years to come. Certainly, companies with products and services to sell will find a way to get audiences to notice what they have to offer. Consumers, on the other hand, will still turn to "media" to find products and services (or will they?) and then make choices among those that are available. This "model" has been in place since the 1800s, and it is still viable. But the world is changing.

What is being debated does not question the fundamental seller–buyer model. Rather, the debate that is taking place focuses on *how* companies will get in front of consumers, and *what means* consumers will use to find out what is available. Said another way, there is considerable debate and discussion in the advertising and marketing community today about two issues: "fragmented marketplace" and "consumer control."

These are not new topics. Ever since the advent of cable TV in the mid-1980s, satellite TV in the early 1990s, and cellular phones and XM radio in the early 2000s, advertisers and their ad agencies have been struggling to keep up with the number of different ways consumers get information. Increasingly, these technologies have allowed consumers to choose how, where, and when they consume programming and information ("content"). This has shifted the control of advertising delivery to consumers rather than the media outlets of just a few years ago.

Beginning around the year 2000, consumers were spending more of their time, and more of their money, on media that were funded by consumer spending, not advertising. In the next few years, this trend accelerated at a geometric pace. At the same time, AOL Time Warner, then the world's largest media company, was talking about its ability to sell products directly to consumers on a personal, one-to-one basis. By the fall of 2001, the dotcom explosion had occurred, the U.S. economy was shaken by the terrorist attacks of September 11, and the advertising industry was headed for one of the worst recessions it ever suffered.

For those of us in the advertising business then, the years 2002 and 2003 will not be easily forgotten. Advertising spending came to what appeared to be a grinding halt. Because of these conditions, many ad agencies were forced to close their doors or lay off staff. The inherent optimism that is part of the advertising business made most managers believe things would turn around eventually. Things did turn around to some degree, but the face of advertising and media was forever changed. At the same time, marketers were not immune to the marketplace changes that were affecting ad agencies.

Consumers, after getting a taste of what it was like to access media content on demand, clearly liked the convenience and control. In addition, the Internet had taught them that most content could be accessed for free as long as they could put up with annoying banner ads that were really electronic commercials of short duration. TiVo made it possible to bypass the 30-second television commercial. Clearly, content was beginning to lose control over media consumption because viewers didn't have to watch programming at only one time. And technology was making it possible to almost completely avoid seeing what had made the content possible in the first place: advertising. Many advertising and marketing gurus say that this is when the old paradigm shifted, and when the consumer became king.

What followed was the incredible growth of a subset of online advertising: search. This gave further validity to the notion that consumers were now controlling their individual media content and advertising. Instead of media companies pushing content to consumers, consumers were pulling the content they wanted, when they wanted it. And technology made it possible to pull that content to the media platform of the consumer's choice. Search had become an alternative way for consumers to control how they accessed advertising content.

In the advertising-supported model of media that has been in place for more than 100 years, advertisers pay for media and consumers watch their ads. Online searching, however, and emerging TV-based search are challenging this model by enabling consumers to bypass advertisers and their advertising messages.

MEET A NEW MEDIA CONSUMER

Let's call him Nathan. Nathan watches television occasionally, but he spends more time with his computer. He checks his favorite news website almost hourly. He does his shopping and much of his ordering of goods directly from the desk where his computer sits.

In today's Wi-Fi environment, sometimes Nathan does this from the park or from a local coffee house using his laptop as a combination yellow-pages directory, telephone, notepad, and credit card all wrapped into one unit. He reads magazines, but they are very narrow titles with a lot of technical computer content.

At the same time, when Nathan decides he wants to "access content" (as opposed to "watch television"), he might use online file sharing that will give him virtually all the same content available on over-the-air or cable TV, on demand, when and where he wants it. At the writing of this case, BitTorrent and Gnutella were two of the most used online file-sharing portals. These file-sharing exchanges also make it possible for Nathan to view movies and other on-demand materials when and where he chooses. While this has raised many legal issues and implications for media rights holders, and while Nathan is one of a growing "new media consumer" base, technology is now beginning to threaten the very core of Madison Avenue and its approach to paid media advertising.

The ad agency world can see what is coming. This is why ad agencies, advertisers, and even the TV networks have been talking about branded entertainment and product placement. What the Nathans of today have told agencies is that ads have to be integrated directly into the media content he watches and be relevant to him, or it has to be content that he seeks out directly as part of a product or service he is interested in.

MORE TECHNOLOGICAL CHANGE

"Video platforms" is a term heard more and more. It refers to TV, broadband video, cell-phone screens, and whatever comes next. As new technologies emerge, these video platforms are likely to converge, changing once again the environment in which people seek and receive media content.

One of the many companies exploring this aggressively has been Publicis Media. Under the guidance of leaders with titles like chief innovation officer, Publicis has been studying video convergence to prepare for the day when "the Internet becomes television" and when people start using TV like the Internet. Publicis thinks the convergence of these two platforms will lead to a seamless on-demand and ultimately fragmented video advertising marketplace, in which ad messages are planned not to reach households or even demographics, but individuals. In this environment, Publicis thinks that the traditional concepts of target-based media planning will become obsolete. The new focus of media planning, Publicis thinks, will be on "re-aggregating audiences."

What are "re-aggregated audiences"? They are individuals who have been combined into new audiences (targets) because of factors other than traditional media demographic identification. In markets where cable TV operators can deliver addressable TV ads, ads can then be sent to *individuals*, not demographic targets. If this sounds like Direct Response TV, it is. *Really* direct. In this world, cost-per-thousand (CPM) data and cost-per-point data (CPP) will be far less important than response rates and conversion rates. In this world, TV will be like the Internet, and vice versa.

Addressable TV is a slowly emerging, expensive trend. No one knows if it will catch on or not. But technology is one thing, and consumers are another. Clearly, each continues to change in ways that are good and bad as far as advertising agencies are concerned.

FRAGMENTED MEDIA AND CONSUMER CONTROL

Fragmented media and consumer control are two trends that will continue to pose challenges for traditional advertising and media agencies. They will also pose challenges to marketers as they seek new and better ways to reach consumers. Consumers have always purchased products and services on both a rational and emotional basis. The smartest marketers have always viewed their marketing as a *conversation* with their customers, in which they could learn about changing customer wants, needs, and perceptions. This has allowed marketers like Procter & Gamble to develop a customer focus and has led to many new and innovative products.

The question for marketers is this: if the traditional model of delivering information and emotional content in the form of advertising has been superceded by one where the consumer now has control and chooses what marketing information he or she "consumes," will marketers have to find a new model beyond the traditional idea of the "marketing mix"—product, price, promotion, and place—to create preference and brand loyalty? Those of you reading this case who go on to work in the marketing, advertising, and media world will be the ones who will have to figure this out.

Agencies and employees who do not adapt will be out of business or unemployed. Already a number of ad agencies understand that what was called nontraditional advertising and marketing yesterday is really not that today. The core of advertising and marketing is not about ads, or TV, or traditional thinking; it is all about big ideas, wherever they come from, and the ability to spread original thinking across multiple media platforms.

Firms like BBH, Fallon, Mother, Naked, Strawberry Frog, and Taxi are doing this. All are great examples of gutsy, bold, risk-taking "ad agencies" that are determined to be successful. At the same time, companies such as Procter & Gamble, Burger King, and Mini-Cooper are engaging new thinking to meet the changing world of marketing. Can you name any others?

QUESTIONS

1. How unique do you think Nathan is in his media habits?
2. What do you think about "consumer control"?
3. What additional media fragmentation can you identify?
4. What is the difference between accessing content and watching television?
5. Is there a future for general-purpose magazines? Is there a future for newspapers? Explain.

6. What has the iPod done to radio and radio advertising?
7. What is product placement? Is it effective? Why, or why not?
8. Do you think there is a place for emotional advertising? Or has factual content made emotional advertising old-fashioned? Explain.
9. What do you think will be the next great fad or trend in marketing and advertising?
10. What do you think the future will require of marketers?
11. Do you think marketing in the future will be different, or will there just be new terms and phrases to describe it? Explain.
12. Is the traditional "marketing mix" notion—price, place, product, and promotion—still viable? Why, or why not?

EDD APPLEGATE is a professor in the School of Journalism, College of Mass Communication, Middle Tennessee State University, in Murfreesboro. He earned his doctorate from Oklahoma State University in 1984. Applegate teaches courses in advertising, including Survey of Advertising, Advertising Copywriting, Advertising Management, and Advertising Campaigns. He has written and edited several books, including *Strategic Copywriting: How to Create Effective Advertising* (2004), *Personalities and Products: A Historical Perspective on Advertising in America* (Contributions to the Study of Mass Media and Communications, Number 53) (1998), and *The Ad Men and Women: A Biographical Dictionary of Advertising* (1994). He has contributed almost 60 entries and chapters to encyclopedias and books. He has written more than 20 refereed articles for scholarly journals and proceedings and has presented more than 20 refereed papers at academic conferences.

ART JOHNSEN, the "fire marshall" at Locomotion Creative, in Nashville, Tennessee, began his marketing and advertising career after earning an MBA from the Darden School at the University of Virginia in 1972. His first job was in marketing for Wachovia Bank in Winston-Salem, North Carolina. In this position, he interacted with the bank's advertising agency—Long, Haymes & Carr, also located in Winston-Salem. This experience led him to seek, in 1978, his first ad agency position: account executive with Lewis Advertising, a full-service advertising agency in Rocky Mount, North Carolina. In 1982 he was promoted to vice president and account supervisor. While at Lewis, he worked on the Hardee's, Peoples Bank, and Perdue Farms accounts. In 1987 he moved to Nashville and joined the Buntin Group. As a management supervisor working in account service, he worked with Cracker Barrel Old Country Store and Diabetes Treatment Centers of America.

In 1994 he joined the Bohan Agency as director of client services. In 1998, while working at Bohan, he joined three others to found a branding and design company named Creative Works. In 2003 the company's name was changed to Locomotion Creative, and he moved from being the chief operating officer of Bohan to the fire marshall of Locomotion Creative. At Locomotion Creative, everyone gets to choose his or her title. When he put out a fire in the company's microwave oven, he forever became "The Fire Marshall."

In his spare time, Johnsen has served as an adjunct professor at Belmont University, Middle Tennessee State University, Tennessee Tech, and Vanderbilt University.